Andrew P.  Peabody

## Of the Hawaiian Mission

And the  Missions to Micronesia and the Marquesas Islands

Andrew P. Peabody

**Of the Hawaiian Mission**
*And the Missions to Micronesia and the Marquesas Islands*

ISBN/EAN: 9783744713108

Printed in Europe, USA, Canada, Australia, Japan

Cover: Foto ©Lupo / pixelio.de

More available books at **www.hansebooks.com**

# HISTORICAL SKETCH

## OF THE

# HAWAIIAN MISSION,

### AND THE MISSIONS TO

# MICRONESIA AND THE MARQUESAS ISLANDS.

BY

PROF. S. C. BARTLETT, D.D.

———

BOSTON:
AMERICAN BOARD OF COMMISSIONERS FOR FOREIGN MISSIONS.
1869.

# SKETCH OF THE HAWAIIAN MISSION.

In the year 1809, a dark skinned boy was found weeping on the door-steps at Yale College. His name was Henry Obookiah (Opukahaia); and he came from the Sandwich Islands. In a civil war, his father and mother had been slain before his eyes; and when he fled with his infant brother on his back, the child was killed with a spear, and he was taken prisoner. Lonely and wretched, the poor boy, at the age of fourteen, was glad to come, with Captain Brintnell, to New Haven. He thirsted for instruction; and he lingered round the College buildings, hoping in some way to gratify his burning desire. But when at length all hope died out, he sat down and wept. The Rev. Edwin W. Dwight, a resident graduate, found him there, and kindly took him as a pupil.

In the autumn of that year came another resident graduate to New Haven, for the purpose of awakening the spirit of missions. It was Samuel J. Mills. Obookiah told Mills his simple story — how the people of Hawaii " are very bad; they pray to gods made of wood;" and he longs "to learn to read this Bible, and go back there and tell them to pray to God up in heaven." Mills wrote to Gordon Hall, " What does this mean? Brother Hall, do you understand it? Shall he be sent back unsupported, to attempt to reclaim his countrymen? Shall we not rather consider these southern islands a proper place for the establishment of a mission?" Mills took Obookiah to his own home in Torringford, and thence to Andover for a two years' residence; after which the young man found his way to the grammar school at Litchfield, and when it was opened, in 1817, to the Foreign Mission School at Cornwall, Conn. At Litchfield he became acquainted and intimate with Samuel Ruggles, who about this time (1816) resolved to accompany him to his native island with the gospel.

In the same vessel which brought Obookiah to America, came two other Hawaiian lads, William Tennooe (Kanui) and Thomas Hopu. After roving lives of many years, in 1815 they were both converted — Tennooe at New Haven, and Hopu after he had removed from New Haven to Torringford. Said Hopu, after his conversion, " I want my poor countrymen to know about Christ." These young men, too, had been the objects of much personal interest in New Haven ; and in the following June, during the sessions of the General Association in that city, a meeting was called by some gentlemen to discuss the project of a Foreign Mission School. An organization was effected under the American Board that autumn, at the house of President Dwight, three months before his death. Next year the school opened. Its first principal was Mr. Edwin Dwight, who found Obookiah in tears at Yale College, and among its first pupils were Obookiah, Tennooe, Hopu, and two other Hawaiian youths, with Samuel Ruggles and Elisha Loomis.

But Obookiah was never to carry the gospel in person to his countrymen. God had a wiser use for him. In nine months from the opening of the Mission School, he closed a consistent Christian life with a peaceful Christian death. The lively interest which had been gathering round him was profoundly deepened by his end and the memoir of his life, and was rapidly crystallizing into a mission. Being dead, he yet spoke with an emphasis and an eloquence that never would have been given him in his life. The touching story drew legacies from the dying, and tears, prayers, donations, and consecrations from the living. " O what a wonderful thing," he once had said, " that the hand of Divine Providence has brought me here from that heathenish darkness. And here I have found the name of the Lord Jesus in the Holy Scriptures, and have read that his blood was shed for many. My poor countrymen, who are yet living in the region and shadow of death ! — I often feel for them in the night season, concerning the loss of their souls. May the Lord Jesus dwell in my heart, and prepare me to go and spend the remainder of my life with them. But not my will, but thine, O Lord, be done."

The will of the Lord was done. The coming to America was a more " wonderful thing" than he thought. His mantle fell on other shoulders, and in two years more a missionary band was ready for the Sandwich Islands. Hopu, Tennooe, and John Honoree, natives of the islands, were to be accompanied by Hiram Bingham and Asa Thurston, young graduates of Andover, Dr. Thomas Holman, a young physician, Daniel Chamberlain, a substantial farmer, Samuel Whitney, mechanic and teacher, Samuel Ruggles, catechist and teacher, and

Elisha Loomis, printer and teacher. All the Americans were accompanied by their wives, and Mr. Chamberlain by a family of five children. Mr. Ruggles seems to have been the first to determine upon joining the mission, and Mr. Loomis had been a member of the Mission School. With this company went also George Tamoree (Kamaulii), who had been a wanderer in America for fourteen years, to return to his father, the subject king of Kauai.

The ordination of Messrs. Bingham and Thurston, at Goshen, Conn., drew from the surrounding region a large assembly, among whom were a great number of clergymen, and nearly all the members of the Mission School, now thirty or more in number; and " liberal offerings " for the mission came in " from all quarters." A fortnight later, the missionary band were organized at Boston into a church of seventeen members; public services were held Friday evening and Saturday forenoon, in the presence of " crowded " houses, at the Park-street Church; and on the Sabbath, six hundred communicants sat with them at the table of the Lord. " The occasion," says the " Panoplist " of that date, " was one of the most interesting and solemn which can exist in this world.". On Saturday, the 23rd of October, 1819, a Christian assembly stood upon Long Wharf, and sang, " Blest be the tie that binds." There was a prayer by Dr. Worcester, a farewell speech by Hopu, a song by the missionaries, " When shall we all meet again ; " and a fourteen oared barge swiftly conveyed the little band from their weeping friends to the brig " Thaddeus," which was to carry the destiny of the Hawaiian Islands.

While the missionaries are on their way, let us take a look at the people whom they were going to reclaim. The ten islands of the Hawaiian group — an area somewhat less than Massachusetts — were peopled by a well formed, muscular race, with olive complexions and open countenances, in the lowest stages of barbarism, sensuality, and vice. The children went stark naked till they were nine or ten years old ; and the men and women wore the scantiest apology for clothing, which neither sex hesitated to leave in the hut at home before they passed through the village to the surf. The king came more than once from the surf to the house of Mr. Ruggles with his five wives, all in a state of nudity ; and on being informed of the impropriety, he came the next time dressed — with a pair of silk stockings and a hat ! The natives had hardly more modesty or shame than so many animals. Husbands had many wives, and wives many husbands ; and exchanged with each other at pleasure. The most revolting forms of vice, as Captain Cook had occasion to know, were practiced in open sight. When a foreign vessel came to the harbor, the women would swim to it in flocks for the vilest of purposes. Two thirds of all the children, probably, were destroyed in infancy — strangled or buried alive.

The nation practiced human sacrifice; and there is a cord now at the Missionary Rooms, Chicago, with which one high priest had strangled twenty-three human victims. They were a race of perpetual thieves; even kings and chiefs kept servants for the special purpose of stealing. They were wholesale gamblers, and latterly drunkards. Thoroughly savage, they seemed almost destitute of fixed habits. When food was plenty, they would take six or seven meals a day, and even rise in the night to eat; at other times they would eat but once a day, or perhaps go almost fasting for two or three days together. And for purposes of sleep the day and the night were much alike. Science they had none; no written language, nor the least conception of any mode of communicating thought but by oral speech.

A race that destroyed their own children had little tender mercy. Sons often buried their aged parents alive, or left them to perish. The sick were abandoned to die of want and neglect. Maniacs were stoned to death. Captives were tortured and slain. The whole system of government and religion was to the last degree oppressive. The lands, their products, and occupants, were the property of the chiefs and the king. The persons and power of the high chiefs were protected by a crushing system of restrictions, called *tabus*. It was tabu and death for a common man to let his shadow fall upon a chief, to go upon his house, enter his enclosure, or wear his *kapa*, to stand when the king's *kapa* or his bathing water was carried by, or his name mentioned in song. In these and a multitude of other ways, "men's heads lay at the feet of the king and the chiefs." In like manner it was tabu for a woman to eat with her husband, or to eat fowl, pork, cocoanut, or banana — things offered to the idols — and death was the penalty. The priest, too, came in with his tabus and his exactions for his idols. There were six principal gods with names, and an indefinite number of spirits. Whatsoever the priest demanded for the god — food, a house, land, human sacrifice — must be forthcoming. If he pronounced a day tabu, the man who was found in a canoe, or even enjoying the company of his family, died. If any one made a noise when prayers were saying, or if the priest pronounced him irreligious, he died. When a temple was built, and the people had finished the toil, some of them were offered in sacrifice. In all these modes, the oppression of the nation was enormous.

The race had once been singularly healthy. They told the first missionaries — an exaggeration, of course — that formerly they died only of old age. But foreign sailors had introduced diseases, reputable, and especially disreputable ; and now, between the desolations of war, infanticide, and infamous diseases widely spread by general licentiousness, the nation was rapidly wasting away.

Such was the forbidding race on whom the missionaries were to try the power of the cross. " Probably none of you will live to witness the downfall of idolatry," — so said the Rev. Mr. Kellogg to Mr. Ruggles, as they took breakfast together at East Windsor, the morning before he left home. And so thought, no doubt, the whole community. But God's thoughts are not as our thoughts.

Hopu called up his friend Ruggles at one o'clock on a moonlight night (March 31) to get the first glimpse of Hawaii ; and at daybreak the snow-capped peak of Mauna Kea was in full view. A few hours more, and Hopu pointed out the valley where he was born. A boat is put off, with Hopu and others in it, which encounters some fishermen, and returns. As the boat nears the vessel, Hopu is seen swinging his hat in the air ; and as soon as he arrives within hail, he shouts, " Oahu's idols are no more ! " On coming aboard, he brings the thrilling news that the old king Kamehameha is dead ; that Liholiho, his son, succeeds him ; that the images of the gods are all burned ; that the men are all " Inoahs," — they eat with the women ; that but one chief was killed in settling the government, and he for refusing to destroy his gods. Next day, the message was confirmed. Kamehamcha, a remarkable man, had passed away. On his deathbed, he asked an American trader to tell him about the Americans' God ; but, said the native informant, in his broken English, " He no tell him anything." All the remaining intelligence was also true. The missionaries wrote in their journal, " Sing, O heavens, for the Lord hath done it." The brig soon anchored in Kailua Bay, the king's residence ; and a fourteen days' consultation between the king and chiefs, followed. Certain foreigners opposed their landing ; " they had come to conquer the islands." " Then," said the chiefs, " they would not have brought their women." The decision was favorable. Messrs. Bingham, Loomis, Chamberlain, and Honoree, go to Oahu ; and Messrs. Ruggles and Whitney accompany the young Tamoree to his father, the subject king of Kauai. The meeting of father and son was deeply affecting. The old king, for his son's sake, adopted Mr. Ruggles also, as his son, and gave him a tract of land, with the power of a chief. He prepared him a house, soon built a school-house and chapel, and followed him with acts of friendship which were of great benefit to the mission while the king lived, and after his death. He himself became a hopeful convert, and in 1824 died in the faith.

And now the missionaries settled down to their work. They had found a nation sunk in ignorance, sensuality and vice, and nominally without a religion — though, really, still in the grasp of many of their old superstitions. The old religion had been discarded chiefly on account of its burdensomeness. We cannot here recount all the agencies, outer and inner, which brought about this remarkable convulsion. But no religious motives seem to have had any special power. Indeed, King Liholiho was intoxicated when he dealt to the system its finishing stroke, by compelling his wives to eat pork. And by a Providence as remarkable as inscrutable, the high priest threw his whole weight into the scale. Into this opening, thus signally furnished by the hand of God, the missionaries entered, with wonder and gratitude. The natives educated in America proved less serviceable than was expected. Tennooe was soon excommunicated; although in later years he recovered, and lived and died a well-reputed Christian. Hopu and Honoree, while they continued faithful, had partly lost their native tongue, lacked the highest skill as interpreters, and naturally failed in judgment. Hopu, at the opening of the first revival, was found busy in arranging the inquirers on his right hand and his left hand, respectively, as they answered yes or no to the single question, " Do you love your enemies? " and was greatly disturbed at being interrupted.

The king and the chiefs, with their families, were the first pupils. They insisted on the privilege. Within three months, the king could read the English language; and in six months, several chiefs could both read and write. The missionaries devoted themselves vigorously to the work of reducing the native speech to writing; and in less than two years, the first sheet of a native spelling-book was printed — followed by the second, however, only after the lapse of six months. From time to time, several accessions of laborers were received from America, and various changes of location took place. The first baptized native was Keopuolani, the mother of the king; and others of the high chiefs were among the earlier converts. The leading personages, for the most part, showed much readiness to adopt the suggestions of the missionaries. In 1824, the principal chiefs formally agreed to recognize the Sabbath, and to adopt the ten commandments as the basis of government. They also soon passed a law forbidding females to visit the ships for immoral purposes.

The gravest obstacles encountered, came from vile captains and crews of English and American vessels. They became ferocious towards the influences and the men that checked their lusts. The British whale-ships Daniel, and John Palmer, and the American armed schooner Dolphin, commanded by Lieutenant Percival, were prominent in open outrage. The house of missionary Richards was twice assailed by the ruffians of the ship Daniel, encouraged by their captain. On one occasion, they came and demanded his influence to repeal the law against prostitution. On his refusal, they, in the presence of his feeble wife, threatened, with horrid oaths, to destroy his property, his house, his life, and the lives of all his family. Two days after, forty men returned, with a black flag, and armed with knives, repeating the demand. The chiefs at length called out a company of two hundred men, armed with muskets and spears, and drove them off. The crew of the Dolphin, with knives and clubs, on the Sabbath, assailed a small religious assembly of chiefs, gathered at the house of one of their number, who was sick. Mr. Bingham, who was also present, fell into their hands, on his way to protect his house, and barely escaped with his life from the blow of a club and the thrust of a knife, being rescued by the natives. A mob of English and American whalemen, in October, 1826, started for the house of Mr. Richards, at Lahaina, with the intention of taking his life. Not finding him, they pillaged the town; while all the native women, from a population of 4,000, fled from their lust, for refuge in the mountains. A year later, the family of Mr. Richards took refuge in the cellar, from the cannon-balls of the John Palmer, which passed over the roof of the house. When printed copies of the ten commandments were about to be issued, this class of men carried their opposition, with threats, before the king. At Honolulu, while the matter was pending, Mr. Ruggles was approached by an American captain, bearing the satirical name of Meek, who flourished his dagger, and angrily declared himself ready " to bathe his hands in the heart's blood of every missionary who had any thing to do with it." At one time, twenty-one sailors came up the hill, with clubs, threatening to kill the missionaries unless they were furnished with women. The natives gathering for worship, immediately thronged round the house so thick that they were intimidated, and sneaked away. At another time, fourteen of them surrounded him, with the same demand; but were frightened off by the resolute bearing of the noble chief Kapiolani — a majestic woman, six feet high — who, arriving at the instant, swung her umbrella over her head, with the crisp words, " Be off in a moment, or I will have every one of you in irons." She was the same Christian heroine who, in 1824, broke the terrible spell which hung over the volcano Kilauea, by venturing down into the crater, in defiance of the goddess Pele, hurling stones into the boiling lake, and worshiping Jehovah on its black ledge.

It is easy to understand why a certain class of captains and sailors have always pronounced the Sandwich Islands Mission a wretched failure.

The missionaries labored on undaunted. Eight years from their landing found them at work, some thirty-two in number, with 440 native teachers, 12,000 Sabbath hearers, and 26,000 pupils in their schools. At this time, about fifty natives, including Kaahumanu, the Queen Regent, and many of the principal chiefs, were members of the church. And now, in the year 1828, the dews of heaven began to fall visibly upon the mission. For two or three years, the way had been preparing. Kaahumanu, converted in 1828, and several other high chiefs, had thrown themselves vigorously and heartily into the work. "They made repeated tours around all the principal islands," says Mr. Dibble, "assembling the people from village to village, and delivering addresses day after day, in which they prohibited immoral acts, enjoined the observance of the Sabbath, encouraged the people to learn to read, and exhorted them to turn to God, and to love and obey the Saviour of sinners." "The effect was electrical — pervading at once every island of the group, every obscure village and district, and operating with immense power on all grades and conditions of society. The chiefs gave orders to the people to erect houses of worship, to build school-houses, and to learn to read — they readily did so; to listen to the instructions of the missionaries — they at once came in crowds for that purpose." About this time, too, (May, 1825,) the remains of King Liholiho and his wife were brought back from their unfortunate expedition to England, where they died from the measles. Their attending chiefs filled the ears of the people with what they saw in England; and Lord Byron, commander of the British frigate which brought the remains, gave an honorable testimony to the missionaries.

These various influences caused a great rush to hear the Word of God. The people would come regularly, fifty or sixty miles, traveling the whole of Saturday, to attend Sabbath worship; and would gather in little companies, from every point of the compass, like the tribes as they went up to Jerusalem. Meanwhile, the printed word was circulated throughout the villages.

At length the early fruits appeared. In the year 1828, a gracious work began, simultaneously and without communication, in the islands of Hawaii, Oahu, and Maui. It came unexpectedly. The transactions at Kaavaroa (Hawaii) well illustrate the work. Mr. Ruggles was away from home, with Mr. Bishop, on an excursion to visit the schools of the island. They had been wrecked, and had swum ashore. Two natives who were sent home for shoes and clothing, brought a message from Mrs. Ruggles to her husband, requesting his immediate return, for " strange things were happening — the natives were coming in companies, inquiring what they should do to be saved." He hastened back, and found the house surrounded from morning till night, and almost from night till morning: A company of ten or twenty would be received into the house, and another company would wait their turn at the gate. So it went on for weeks, and even months, and the missionaries could get no rest or refreshment, except as they called in Kapiolani and others of the converted chiefs, to relieve them. Mr. and Mrs. Ruggles had the names of 2,500 inquirers on their books. With multitudes, it was, no doubt, but sympathy or fashion ; but there were also a large number of real inquirers, and many hopeful conversions. All the converts were kept in training classes a year, before they were admitted to the church, and then only on the strictest examination. During the two following years, 350 persons were received to communion at the several stations. For a time, the work seemed to lull again. But in 1836, the whole aspect of the field was so inviting that the Board sent out a strong missionary reinforcement of thirty-two. persons, male and female.

At this time, and for the following year, the hearts of the missionaries were singularly drawn out in desires and prayers for the conversion, not only of the Islands, but of America and of the world. And scarcely had the new laborers been assigned to their places, and learned the language, when (in 1838) there began and continued, for six years, one of the most remarkable awakenings that the world has ever witnessed. All hearts seemed tender. Whenever the Word was preached, conviction and conversions followed. The churches roused up to self-examination and prayer ; the stupid listened ; the vile and groveling learned to feel ; the congregations became immense, and sometimes left their churches for the open air, and the prayer-meetings left the lecture-room for the body of the church. There were congregations of four, five and six thousand persons. The missionaries preached from seven to twenty times a week ; and the sense of guilt in the hearers often broke forth in groans and loud cries. Probably many indiscretions were committed, and there were many spurious conversions. But, after all allowances, time showed that a wonderful work was wrought. During the six years from 1838 to 1843, inclusive, twenty-seven thousand persons were admitted to the churches. In some instances, the crowds to be baptized on a given Sabbath required extraordinary modes of baptism; and Mr. Coan is said to have sprinkled water with a brush upon the candidates, as they came before him in throngs.

The next twenty years added more than 20,000 other members to the churches, making the whole number received up to 1863, some 50,000 souls. Many of these had then been excommunicated — in some instances, it was thought, too hastily; many thousand had gone home to heaven; and in 1863, some 20,000 still survived in connection with the churches.

At length came the time when the Islands were to be recognized as nominally a Christian nation, and the responsibility of their Christian institutions was to be rolled off upon themselves. In June, 1863, Dr. Anderson, Senior Secretary of the American Board, met with the Hawaiian Evangelical Association to discuss this important measure. After twenty-one days of debate, the result was reached with perfect unanimity, and the Association agreed to assume the responsibility which had been proposed to them. This measure was consummated by the Board in the autumn following, and those stations no longer looked to the American churches for management and control. "The mission has been, as such, disbanded and merged in the community."

On the 15th of January, 1864, at Queen's Hospital, Honolulu, died William Kanui, (Tennooe,) aged sixty-six years, the last of the native youth who gave rise to the mission and accompanied the first missionaries. He had wandered — had been excommunicated — and was restored; and after many years of faithful service he died in the triumph of faith. In his last sickness he used "to recount the wonderful ways" in which God had led him. "The names of Cornelius, Mills, Beecher, Daggett, Prentice, Griffin, and others were often on his lips;" and he went, no doubt, to join them all above. God had spared his life to see the whole miraculous change that had lifted his nation from the depths of degradation to civilization and Christianity. Could the spirit of Henry Obookiah have stood in Honolulu soon after the funeral of Kanui, he would have hardly recognized his native island except by its great natural landmarks. He would have seen the city of Honolulu, once a place of grass huts and filthy lanes, now marked by substantial houses and sidewalks, and a general air of civilization; a race of once naked savages decently attired and living, some of them, in comparative refinement; a nation of readers, whom he left without an alphabet; Christian marriage firmly established in place of almost promiscuous concubinage; property in the interior, exposed with absolute security for an indefinite time, where formerly nothing was safe for an hour; the islands dotted with a hundred capacious church edifices, built by native hands, some of them made of stone, most of them with bells; a noble array of several hundred common schools, two female seminaries, a normal school for natives, a high school that furnished the first scholar to one of the classes in Williams College; a theological seminary and twenty-nine native preachers, besides eighteen male and female missionaries sent to the Marquesas Islands; near twenty thousand living church members; a government with a settled constitution, a legislature, and courts of justice, and avowing the Christian religion to be " the established national religion of the Hawaiian Islands."

These facts exhibit the bright and marvelous aspect of the case. But, of course, they have their drawbacks. The Sandwich Islands are not Paradise, nor even America. The stage of civilization is, as it must be, far below that of our own country. The old habits still shade into the new. Peculiar temptations to intemperance and licentiousness come down by inheritance. Foreign interventions and oppositions have been and still are grave hindrances. Church members but fifty years removed from a state of brutalism, can not and do not show the stability, intelligence, and culture of those who inherit the Christian influences of a thousand years.

But the amazing transformation of the islands is a fact that depends not alone on the estimates of the missionaries, or of the Board that employed them. The most generous testimonies have come from other sources. The Rev. F. S. Rising, of the American Church Missionary Society, explored the Islands in 1866, for the express purpose of testing the question. He visited nearly every mission station, examined the institutions — religious, educational, social; made the personal acquaintance of the missionaries of all creeds, and conversed with persons of every profession and social grade. And he writes to the Secretary of the American Board: " The deeper I pushed my investigations, the stronger became my conviction, that what had been on your part necessarily an experimental work in modern missions had, under God, proved an eminent success. Every sunrise brought me new reasons for admiring the power of divine grace, which can lift the poor out of the dust, and set him among princes. Every sunsetting gave me fresh cause to bless the Lord for that infinite love which enables us to bring to our fellow-men such rich blessings as your missionaries have bestowed on the Hawaiian Islands. To me it seemed marvelous, that in comparatively so few years, the social, political, and religious life of the nation should have

undergone so radical and blessed a change as it had. Looking at
the kingdom of Hawaii-nei as it to-day has its recognized place
among the world's sovereignties, I can not but see in it one of the
brightest trophies of the power of the cross." "What of Hawaiian
Christianity? I would apply to it the same test by which we
measure the Christianity of our own and other lands. There are
certain outward signs which indicate that it has a high place in the
national respect, conscience, and affection. Possessing these visible
marks, we declare of any country that it is Christian. The Hawaiian
kingdom, for this reason, is properly and truly called so. The constitution recognizes the Christian faith as the religion of the nation.
The Bible is found in almost every hut. Prayer — social, family,
and individual — is a popular habit. The Lord's day is more sacredly
observed than in New York. Churches of stone or brick dot the
valleys and crown the hill-tops, and have been built by the voluntary
contributions of the natives. There the Word is preached and the
sacraments administered. Sunday schools abound. The contributions of the people for religious uses are very generous, and there is
a native ministry, growing in numbers and influence, girded for
carrying on the work so well begun. The past history of the Hawaiian mission abounds with bright examples [of individual right-
eousness], like Kaahumanu and Kapiolani, and some were pointed
out to me as I went to and fro. They were at one time notoriously
wicked. Their lives are manifestly changed. They are striving to
be holy in their hearts and lives. They are fond of the Bible, of
the sanctuary and prayer. Their theology may be crude, but their
faith in Christ is simple and tenacious. And when we see some such
in every congregation, we know that the work has not been altogether
in vain." In 1860, Richard H. Dana, Esq., a distinguished Boston
lawyer, of the Episcopal Church, gave a similar testimony in the
New York "Tribune," during his visit to the Islands. Among other
things, he mentions that "the proportion of inhabitants who can
read and write is greater than in New England;" that they may be
seen "going to school and public worship with more regularity than
the people at home;" that after attending the examination of Oahu
College, he "advised the young men to remain there to the end of
their course [then extending only to the Junior year], as they could
not pass the Freshman and Sophomore years more profitably elsewhere, in my judgment;" that "in no place in the world, that I have
visited, are the rules which control vice and regulate amusement so
strict, yet so reasonable, and so fairly enforced;" that "in the interior it is well known that a man may travel alone with money, through

the wildest spots, unarmed;" and that he "found no hut without its Bible and hymn book in the native tongue; and the practice of family prayer and grace before meat, though it be no more than a calabash of poi and a few dried fish, and whether at home or on a journey, is as common as in New England a century ago."

There is one sad aspect about this interesting people. The population has been steadily declining since they were first discovered. Cook, in 1773, estimated the number of inhabitants at 400,000. This estimate, long thought to be exaggerated, is now supposed to be not far from the truth. But in 1823, wars, infanticide, foreign lust, imported drinks, and disease, had reduced them to the estimated number of 142,000; and in 1830, to the ascertained number of 130,000. In the lapse of a few years after the first visits of foreign vessels, half the population are said to have been swept away with diseases induced or heightened by their unholy intercourse. The mission has done what could be done to save the nation; but the wide taint of infamous disease was descending down the national life, before the missionaries reached the islands; and the flood-gates of intemperance were wide open. They have retarded the nation's decline; but foreign influences have always interfered — and now, perhaps, more than ever. The sale of ardent spirits was once checked, but is now free. The present monarch stands aloof from the policy of some of his predecessors, and from the influence of our missionaries. And the population, reduced to 62,000 in 1866, seems to be steadily declining. The "Pacific Commercial Advertiser," which furnishes the facts, finds the chief cause in the fearful prevalence, still, of vice and crime, which are said to have been increasing of late; and the reason for this increase is "political degradation," and the readiness with which the people now obtain intoxicating drinks. It must be remembered, that "in the height of the whaling season, the number of transient seamen in the port of Honolulu equals half the population of the town;" and the influences they bring, breathe largely of hell. Commercial forces and movements, meanwhile, are changing the islands. The lands are already passing into the hands of foreign capitalists, and the islands are falling into the thoroughfare of the nations.

The proper sequel, therefore, of this grand missionary triumph may be taken away; and the race itself, as a nation, may possibly cease to be. But in no event can the value or the glory of the work achieved be destroyed. Not only will thousands on thousands of human souls thereby have been brought into the kingdom, by the labor of a hundred missionaries, and the expenditure of perhaps a

million of dollars from America ; but a grand experiment will have been
tried before the world, and an imperishable memorial erected for all
time, of what the remedial power of the gospel can accomplish, in
an incredibly short time, upon a most imbruted race.  " Fifty years
ago," says Dr. A. P. Peabody, " the half-reasoning elephant, or the
tractable and troth-keeping dog, might have seemed the peer, or
more, of the unreasoning and conscienceless Hawaiian.  From that
very race, from that very generation, with which the nobler brutes
might have scorned to claim kindred, have been developed the peers
of saints and angels."  And all the more glorious is the movement,
that the nation was sunk so low, and was so rapidly wasting away.
" If the gospel," says Dr. Anderson, " took the people at the lowest
point of social existence — at death's door, when beyond the reach
of all human remedies, with the causes of decline and destruction all
in their most vigorous operation — and has made them a Christian
people, checked the tide of depopulation, and raised the nation so in
the scale of social life, as to have gained for it an acknowledged place
among the nations of the earth, what more wonderful illustration can
there be of its remedial power ? "

The history of the Sandwich Islands will stand forever as the vin-
dication, to the caviler, of the worth of Christian missions, and as a
demonstration to the Christian, of what they might be expected to
accomplish in other lands, if prosecuted with a vigor at all propor-
tioned to the nature and extent of the field, and crowned with the
blessing of God.

As indicating, somewhat, the present condition at the Islands of
that Christian work for which so much effort has been made, it may
be well to add here a few sentences from the Annual Report of the
American Board for 1868 : —

" The Christianity of the Islands has had severe trials of late, from
the attitude of the government, and the opposition of corrupt and
corrupting officials. . . . The gospel is on trial ; the missionaries,
the native pastors, and the faithful followers of Christ in the native
churches and among the foreign population, are deserving of a large
place in the sympathies and prayers of Christian men the world over,
as against such odds — an unfriendly government, the intrigues of the
Papacy and of the Reformed Catholics, the opposition of ungodly
men, who would perpetuate vice and immorality for their own wicked
ends, and the tendency of the natives, not yet fully confirmed in habits
of virtue, to yield to the pressure of evil within and without — they
still press on with the banner of the cross.

" The addition of 827 members to the native churches on profession of faith, the contribution of \$29,023 to various Christian objects, the sending out of new missionaries, the almost entire support of their own Christian institutions, the past year, are evidences that the good work is nobly maintained. . . .

" There are now twenty-six native pastors, settled over as many churches, besides four licensed preachers, having stated charges, all supported by the Hawaiian churches. And there are thirteen Hawaiian missionaries in the Marquesas and in Micronesia, — eight ordained ministers and five licensed preachers."

The following list presents the names of persons who have been sent out by the American Board, in connection with its work at these Islands. It should be noted, however, that quite a number of the children of missionaries, and some other persons, not named in this list, are or have been engaged in educational and evangelizing labors at the Islands, some of them supported wholly or in part by the Board, and others entirely by those for whom they labor. It should also be said, that many of those sent out by the Board, and still living and laboring at the Islands, no longer receive support from the funds of the Board. Those who are now sustained, wholly or in part, by the Board are designated by the letter A against their names. Those known to have died are marked with a * : —

| NAMES. | Sailed for the Mission. | Left or Released. | Died. |
|---|---|---|---|
| Rev. Hiram Bingham. . . . . | Oct. 23, 1819. | 1841 | |
| Mrs. Sybil Bingham.* . . . | " | " | 1848 |
| Rev. Asa Thurston.* . . . . | " | | 1868 |
| Mrs. Lucy G. Thurston. A . . . | " | | |
| Mr. Daniel Chamberlain. . . . | " | 1823 | |
| Mrs. Chamberlain. . . . . . | " | " | |
| Mr. Samuel Whitney.* . . . . | " | | 1845 |
| Mrs. Mercy Whitney. A . . . | " | | |
| Dr. Thomas Holman.* . . . . | " | 1820 | 1821 |
| Mrs. Lucia Holman. . . . . | " | " | |
| Mr. Elisha Loomis. . . . . | " | 1827 | |
| Mrs. Maria T. Loomis. . . . | " | " | |
| Mr. Samuel Ruggles. . . . . | " | 1834 | |
| Mrs. Nancy Ruggles. . . . . | " | " | |
| Rev. Wm. Richards.* . . . . | Nov. 19, 1822. | 1838 | 1847 |
| Mrs. Clarissa Richards.* . . . | " | " | |
| Rev. Chas. S. Stewart. . . . . | " | 1825 | |
| Mrs. Harriet B. Stewart.* . . . | " | " | |
| Rev. Artemas Bishop. . . . . | " | | |
| Mrs. E. E. Bishop.* . . . . | " | " | 1828 |
| Dr. Abraham Blatchley. . . . | " | 1826 | |
| Mrs. Jemima Blatchley. . . . | " | " | |
| Mr. Joseph Goodrich (ordained at the Islands). . . . . . | " | 1836 | |

2

| NAMES. | Sailed for the Mission. | Left or Released. | Died. |
|---|---|---|---|
| Mrs. Goodrich. | Nov. 19, 1822. | 1836 | |
| Mr. James Ely. | " | 1828 | |
| Mrs. Louisa Ely. | " | " | |
| Mr. Levi Chamberlain.* | " | | 1849 |
| Rev. Lorrin Andrews.* | Nov. 3, 1827. | 1842 | 1868 |
| Mrs. Andrews. | " | " | |
| Rev. E. W. Clark. A | " | | |
| Mrs. Mary K. Clark.* | " | | 1857 |
| Rev. J. S. Green. | " | 1842 | |
| Mrs. T. A. Green. | " | " | ' |
| Rev. P. J. Gulick. | " | | |
| Mrs. F. H. Gulick. | " | | |
| Mrs. M. P. Chamberlain. A | " | | |
| Mr. Stephen Shepard.* | " | | 1834 |
| Mrs. M. C. Shepard. | " | 1835 | |
| Dr. G. P. Judd. | " | 1842 | |
| Mrs. L. P. Judd. | " | " | |
| Miss M. C. Ogden. A | " | | |
| Miss Delia Stone (Mrs. Bishop). | " | | |
| Miss Mary Ward (Mrs. Rogers).* | " | | 1834 |
| Rev. Dwight Baldwin, M. D. A | Dec. 28, 1830. | | |
| Mrs. C. F. Baldwin. A | " | | |
| Rev. Sheldon Dibble.* | " | | 1845 |
| Mrs. M. M. Dibble.* | " | | 1837 |
| Mr. Andrew Johnstone. | " | 1836 | |
| Mrs. Johnstone.* | " | " | |
| Rev. Reuben Tinker.* | " | 1840 | |
| Mrs. M. T. Tinker. | " | " | |
| Rev. J. S. Emerson.* | Nov. 26, 1831. | | 1867 |
| Mrs. Ursula S. Emerson. A | " | | |
| Rev. D. B. Lyman. A | " | | |
| Mrs. Sarah J. Lyman. A | " | | |
| Rev. Ephraim Spaulding.* | " | 1837 | 1840 |
| Mrs. Julia Spaulding. | " | " | |
| Rev. W. P. Alexander. A | " | | |
| Mrs. Mary Ann Alexander. A | " | | |
| Rev. Richard Armstrong.* | " | 1849 | 1860 |
| Mrs. Clarissa Armstrong. | " | " | |
| Rev. Cochran Forbes. | " | 1847 | |
| Mrs. Rebecca D. Forbes. | " | " | |
| Rev. H. R. Hitchcock.* | " | | 1855 |
| Mrs. Rebecca Hitchcock. | " | | |
| Rev. Lorenzo Lyons. A | " | | |
| Mrs. Betsey Lyons.* | " | | 1837 |
| Dr. Alonzo Chapin. | " | 1835 | |
| Mrs. Mary Ann Chapin. | " | " | |
| Mr. Ed. H. Rogers.* | " | | 1853 |
| Rev. Benjamin W. Parker. A | Nov. 2, 1832. | | |
| Mrs. Mary E. Parker. A | " | | |
| Rev. Lowell Smith. A | " | | |
| Mrs. Abby W. Smith. A | " | | |
| Mr. Lemuel Fuller. | " | 1833 | |
| Rev. Titus Coan. A | Dec. 5, 1834. | | |
| Mrs. Fidelia C. Coan. A | " | | |
| Mr. Henry Dimond. | " | 1849 | |
| Mrs. Ann M. Dimond. | " | " | |
| Mr. E. O. Hall. | " | " | |
| Mrs. Sarah L. Hall. | " | " | |

| NAMES. | Sailed for the Mission. | Left or Released. | Died. |
|---|---|---|---|
| Miss Lydia Brown.* | Dec. 5, 1834. | | 1865 |
| Miss E. M. Hitchcock* (Mrs. Rogers). | " | | 1857 |
| Rev. Isaac Bliss. | Dec. 4, 1836. | 1841 | |
| Mrs. Emily Bliss. | " | " | |
| Rev. D. T. Conde. | " | 1858 | |
| Mrs. A. L. Conde.* | " | | 1854 |
| Rev. Mark Ives. | " | 1853 | |
| Mrs. Mary A. Ives. | " | " | |
| Rev. Thomas Lafon, M. D. | " | 1840 | |
| Mrs. Sophia L. Lafon. | " | " | |
| Dr. S. L. Andrews. | " | 1849 | |
| Mrs. Parnelly Andrews.* | " | " | 1846 |
| Mr. Amos S. Cooke. | " | 1852 | |
| Mrs. Juliette M. Cooke. | " | " | |
| Mr. Wm. S. Van Duzee. | " | 1839 | |
| Mrs. Oral Van Duzee. | " | " | |
| Mr. Edward Bailey. | " | 1850 | |
| Mrs. Caroline H. Bailey. | " | " | |
| Mr. Abner Wilcox. A | " | | |
| Mrs. Lucy E. Wilcox. A | " | | |
| Mr. Horton O. Knapp.* | " | | 1845 |
| Mrs. Charlotte Knapp. | " | | |
| Mr. Charles McDonald.* | " | | 1839 |
| Mrs. Harriet T. McDonald. | " | | |
| Mr. Edwin Locke.* | " | | 1843 |
| Mrs. Martha L. Locke.* | " | | 1842 |
| Mr. Bethuel Munn. | " | 1842 | |
| Mrs. Louisa Munn.* | " | | 1841 |
| Mr. Samuel N. Castle. | " | 1852 | |
| Mrs. Angelina L. Castle.* | " | | 1840 |
| Mr. Edward Johnson* (ordained after going). | " | | 1867 |
| Mrs. Lois S. Johnson. A | " | | |
| Miss Marcia Smith. | " | 1853 | |
| Miss Lucy G. Smith (Mrs. Lyons). | " | | |
| Rev. Daniel Dole. A | Nov. 14, 1840. | | |
| Mrs. Charlotte C. Dole.* | " | | 1844 |
| Rev. Elias Bond. A | " | | |
| Mrs. Ellen M. Bond. A | " | | |
| Rev. John D. Paris. A | " | | |
| Mrs. Mary C. Paris, A | " | | |
| Mr. William H. Rice.* | " | | 1862 |
| Mrs. Mary S. Rice. A | " | | |
| Rev. Geo. B. Rowell. | May 5, 1841. | 1865 | |
| Mrs. Malvina J. Rowell. | " | " | |
| Dr. James W. Smith. A | " | | |
| Mrs. M. K. Smith. A | " | | |
| Rev. Asa B. Smith. | 1842 | 1846 | |
| Mrs. Smith. | " | " | |
| Mrs. Mary T. Castle. | Nov. 2, 1842. | 1852 | |
| Rev. C. B. Andrews. | Dec. 4, 1843. | | |
| Rev. T. Dwight Hunt. | " | 1849 | |
| Mrs. Mary H. Hunt. | " | " | |
| Rev. John F. Pogue. A | " | | |
| Rev. Eliphalet Whittlesey. | " | 1854 | |
| Mrs. Eliza H. Whittlesey. | " | " | |
| Miss Maria K. Whitney (Mrs. Pogue). A | " | | |
| Rev. Samuel G. Dwight. | Oct. 23, 1847. | " | |

| NAMES. | Sailed for the Mission. | Left or Released. | Died. |
|---|---|---|---|
| Rev. Henry Kinney.* . . . . | Oct. 23, 1847. | | 1854 |
| Mrs. Maria L. Kinney.* . . . | " | | 1858 |
| Dr. C. H. Wetmore. . . . . | Oct. 16, 1848. | 1856 | |
| Mrs. Lucy S. Wetmore. .. . . | " | " | |
| Rev. W. C. Shipman.* . . . . | June 4, 1854. | | 1861 |
| Mrs. Jane S. Shipman. A . . | " | | |
| Rev. Wm. O. Baldwin. . . . . | Nov. 28, 1854. | 1860 | |
| Mrs. Mary P. Baldwin. . . . | " | " | |
| Mr. Wm. A. Spooner. . . . . | April 16, 1855. | " | |
| Mrs. Eliza Ann Spooner. . . | " | " | |
| Rev. Anderson O. Forbes. A . . . | 1857 | | |

In connection with this sketch, it will be proper briefly to refer to operations at the Islands by Roman Catholic, Mormon, and "Reformed Catholic" missionaries, whose efforts have not been without influence upon the prosperity of that evangelizing work which the missionaries of the Board have prosecuted.

### ROMAN CATHOLICS.

Early in the history of the mission (in 1825), a French adventurer, by the name of Rives, left the Islands, and went to France, where, pretending to be a large landholder at the Islands, and to have much influence, he applied for priests to establish a Papal mission. In 1826 the Pope appointed an Apostolic Prefect of the Sandwich Islands. He arrived at Honolulu, with two other priests and four laymen, in July, 1827. They landed privately, in disregard of the law which required foreigners to obtain permission before landing. Ordered to leave, they still remained, in disregard of law, and connected themselves with a chief who was manifesting a disposition to resist the authority of the Regent. Having opened a chapel, it was at once reported that they worshiped images; and the chiefs feared that their old religion, with all its evil tendencies, was about to be revived. Continuing to identify themselves with a party of malcontents, the rulers had much trouble with them, a conspiracy seemed fast ripening, and at length, in April, 1831, the chiefs passed a formal order, requiring these foreign priests, who were there without authority, and who were regarded as abettors of rebellion and promoters of vice, to leave the Islands. Still they did not go, and in December the government fitted out a vessel and sent them to California. In all this the authorities acted upon their own views of what was right and necessary in the case, while the American missionaries discountenanced anything that would be regarded as an interference with religious liberty.

In 1836 another Papal priest came, and was forbidden to remain. He, however, like the former company, evaded repeated orders to leave, and in the spring of 1837 he was joined by two of the banished priests, returned from California. The captains of an English and of a French war vessel now interfered, to prevent their being at once compelled again to depart; but those who had returned from California did leave in the autumn. In December the government forbade the teaching of "the Pope's religion." In July, 1839, the frigate L'Artemise, Captain Laplace, visited Honolulu, and *compelled* the authorities to sign a treaty declaring the Catholic worship free, and giving a site for a Catholic church at Honolulu. A footing was thus forcibly secured for Papal priests and influence, and the report of the American Board for the next year, 1840, states, " The influence of Popery begins to be disastrously seen on the Island of Oahu. It is adverse to learning, religion, morals, and social order. For this very reason, the best part of the native population regard it with dread and aversion. But it could not be expected that all of such a people, just emerging from utter ignorance and idolatry, would see the errors or resist the inticements of the priests thus forced upon the toleration of the government. The Papal religion has maintained its ground, and, according to the report of the bishop a few years since, it would appear that about one third of the population of the Islands profess to be, or at least are claimed as, " Catholics."

## THE MORMONS.

The teachers of doctrines yet more opposed to the gospel plan of salvation reached the Islands about 1850. Writing in February, 1851, Mr. Lyons stated that two Mormons, "an elder and a prophet," from Salt Lake, had appeared on Hawaii, belonging to "a company of ten, scattered in pairs over the Islands." They and others have labored zealously to propagate the Mormon doctrines, but not with great success. When Dr. Anderson visited the Islands, in 1863, he found their principal settlement on Lanai, a small island opposite Lahaina, but gained no reliable information as to their numbers, saying, however, that in 1861, Captain Gibson, "their leading man on the island," writing the Minister of Foreign Affairs, stated their number of adults at 3,580.

## "Reformed Catholics."

Bishop Staley, from England, and two presbyters, belonging to the "High Church," "Ritualistic" portion of the English Established Church, reached Honolulu in October, 1862. Styling themselves "Reformed Catholics," they, and others who have followed them in the same mission, have from the outset pursued a course adverse to the interests of the American mission, and of Evangelical Protestant Christianity; manifesting more sympathy for, and more readiness to fellowship with, the Papal than the Protestant preachers and church, and in their worship, their readings and drapings, and their many ceremonies, approaching far more nearly to the formalism of Rome than to the simplicity of the gospel. But though countenanced by the king, and by others in high places, they seem to have found it difficult to interest very many of the people in their new form of religion. It has been too showy, too much like the Roman Catholic, for their religious tastes and convictions. The precise statistics of the mission cannot be given. Bishop Staley has now been for some time in England, but there are presbyters and "sisters" at the Islands, occupying, it is supposed, four stations at least, — Honolulu, Lahaina, Kona, and Wailuku, — with schools for boys and for girls, as well as preaching services. How many they number, as connected with their church or congregations, is not known.

# SKETCH OF THE MICRONESIA MISSION.

THE mission church must in due time turn missionary. So rightly reasoned the members of the Sandwich Islands mission. Thirty years had elapsed; fifteen hundred dollars a year were collected at the monthly concert; the first native pastor had been ordained by a council of native churches; and in the same year, the members of the mission proposed that Hawaiian Christians should carry the gospel to other islands. The Prudential Committee at Boston warmly approved the proposal. Another year (1850) saw the "Hawaiian Missionary Society" formed at Honolulu.

Two thousand miles away, to the south-west of Honolulu, lie an immense number of islands — two thousand or more — now embraced under the general name of Micronesia — "The Little Islands." Scattered in groups, known by various appellations — Ladrones, Carolines, and the like — they stretch from three degrees south to twenty degrees north of the equator, and were then supposed to contain a population of two hundred thousand. Many of them were built wholly by the coral insect, and lie flat upon the water, while a few of them are basaltic islands, with mountains two or three thousand feet in height. These various groups differ in language and in the details of their customs and superstitions, but agree in the general characteristics of their native occupants. They are the natural homes of indolence and sensuality, of theft and violence. The warmth of the climate renders clothing a superfluity, and houses needless except for shade; while the constant vegetation of the tropics dispenses with accumulated stores of food. A race of tawny savages stalk round almost or quite naked, swim like fish in the waters, or bask in the sunshine on shore. They prove as ready to catch, as vile sailors are to communicate, the vices of civilized lands. Intemperance is an easily besetting sin; and licentiousness is, with rare exceptions, the

(23)

general and almost inradicable pollution of the Pacific Islands. But in the Kingsmill group, the missionaries found a people who, though practicing polygamy, held in honor the chastity of woman.

The attention of the missionaries was turned to three of these groups of islands — the Caroline, the Marshall, or Mulgrave, and the Kingsmill, or Gilbert Islands.

The eastern portion of the Caroline chain was naturally fixed upon as the centre of operations, by reason of the convenient location and healthful climate. Two of these, Kusaie and Ponape, were the first to be occupied. Ponape — or Ascension Island — is a high basaltic island, sixty miles in circumference, surrounded by ten smaller basaltic islands, all inclosed within a coral reef. It rises to the height of 2,850 feet, and has its rivers and waterfalls. The island is a physical paradise, with a delightful climate — in which the range of the thermometer for three years was but seventeen degrees, and with a various and luxuriant vegetation. Among the indigenous products are the breadfruit, banana, cocoanut, taro, sugar-cane, ava, arrowroot, sassafras, sago, wild orange, and mango, with an immense variety of timber trees; while lemons, oranges, pine-apples, coffee, tamarinds, guava, tobacco, and other exotics, thrive abundantly. From the mangrove trees that line the shore, the ground rises by a series of natural terraces; and while twenty varieties of birds fill the air with life, a population of five thousand people are so hidden in the overhanging forests and shrubbery, that, but for an occasional canoe, or a smoke ascending, the passing vessel would scarcely know it to be inhabited. The inhabitants seem to be of Malay descent, and the place was "a moral Sodom."

Kusaie — or Strong's Island — the easternmost of the Carolines, is one of a small cluster, and is about thirty miles in circumference. It rises to the height of 2,000 feet, wooded to the summit; and it then contained some 1,500 people, strongly Asiatic both in look and speech. Here polygamy was unknown, and labor comparatively honorable. Many of the inhabitants, with an unusual quickness of apprehension, had learned of foreigners a kind of broken English before the missionaries arrived; and the "Good King George," as his subjects called him, had, with surprising wisdom, forbidden the tapping of the cocoanut tree for the manufacture of intoxicating drink.

North-east of Kusaie lie the Marshall — sometimes called Mulgrave — Islands; subdivided into the Radack and Ralick — or eastern and western — chains. About thirty principal islands compose the group. They are all of coral formation, but much higher, more fertile and inviting, than the Gilbert group south of them. Majuro, or Arrowsmith, for example, is described as a magnificent island, rising eight or ten feet above the water at the landing-place, sprinkled with forests of breadfruit and pandanus trees, and abounding with cocoanuts and bananas. The population of the whole group was estimated at twelve thousand or upwards, speaking, to some extent, different languages. They had been comparatively uncontaminated by foreign intercourse, from their reputation for ferocity. Several vessels had been cut off by them, and a great number of foreigners killed at different times, in retaliation for ·a former deadly attack upon the natives. The residence of the king and principal chiefs was at Ebon Island. The natives are in some respects superior to many of the Pacific islanders. Their features are sharper, their persons spare and athletic, and their countenances vivacious. The women wear their hair smoothly parted on the forehead, and neatly rolled up in the neck — sometimes adorned with flowers; and their skirts, fine, and beautifully braided and bordered, extend from the waist to the feet. The men exhibit much more skill than is common in this region, and are fond of ornaments. Their comparative intelligence and exemption from foreign influence constituted the inviting aspect of this case; their alleged ferocity, the formidable feature.

Directly south of the Marshall Islands, on both sides of the equator, lie the Kingsmill, or Gilbert Islands. Fifteen or sixteen principal islands, surrounded by a multitude of islets, raised by the coral insect barely above the level of the ocean, contain a population of thirty or forty thousand, speaking mostly a common language, resembling the Hawaiian. The land is densely covered with cocoanut groves. This is the " tree of a thousand uses," furnishing the natives almost "everything they eat, drink, wear, live in, or use in any way." Their hats, clothing, mats and cords are made from its leaves; their houses are built from its timber; they eat the fruit, drink the milk, make molasses and rum from its juice, and manufacture from it immense quantities of oil for use and for sale. Their religion is the loosest system of spirit-worship, without priest, idol, or temple. They practice polygamy. The children go naked for ten or twelve years. The men wear a girdle, and the women a broader mat around them. Their appearance of nudity is relieved by the tattooing, with which they are profusely and skillfully adorned. The considerable population, the unity of origin, faith, and language, and the general resemblance of their speech to the Hawaiian, rendered this group inviting, especially to the Sandwich Island laborers, although its torrid sun, comparatively barren soil, and limited range of vegetation, made it not altogether favorable for the American missionaries' home.

Such was the region to which the gospel was to be carried. On the 18th of November, 1851, missionaries Snow and Gulick, with their wives, left Boston in the Esther May, and two months afterward, Mr. and Mrs. Sturges, in the Snow Squall, for Micronesia by way of the Sandwich Islands. Seven native Hawaiians were ready to join them; but two only, with their wives, were selected for the opening of the mission. The native churches made liberal contributions for their outfit and support. King Kamehameha III. gave them a noble letter of commendation to the Micronesian chiefs. A mission church was organized early in July, 1852, and on the 15th of the same month, just thirty-three years, or one whole generation, from the date of the former parting at Long Wharf in Boston, the like scene took place in the harbor of Honolulu. A crowd of natives thronged the shore as the missionaries put off for the schooner Caroline. On the deck of the schooner there is a prayer in Hawaiian and another in English, a verse of the Missionary Hymn, a shaking of friendly hands; and with a gentle breeze the vessel glides away.

The Caroline arrived at the Gilbert Islands, and on the 21st of August anchored at Kusaie. The missionaries were pleasantly received by " Good King George," in a faded flannel shirt, while his wife sat by in a short cotton gown, and his subjects approached him crouching on their hands and knees. He consented to the mission, gave them supplies, promised them land and a house, and on hearing the thirteenth chapter of Romans, and witnessing their worship, he pronounced both to be " first rate." Messrs. Snow, Opunui, and their wives, commenced their work in this isolated place, where at one time they passed a period of two full years without a letter from America. A fortnight later the Caroline anchored in the land-locked harbor of Ponape, where the king came on board, and, after some conversation, told them it should be " good for them to stop." And here Messrs. Sturges, Gulick, Kaaikaula, and their wives, were soon established in their new home.

In 1854 they were followed by Dr. Pierson and the native Hawaiian, Kanoa. These brethren brought a blessing to the crew of the whaling bark Belle, that carried them; her three mates were converted on the voyage. As they cruised among the Marshall Islands on their way to Kusaie, by a good providence the King's sister — a remarkable woman — took passage from Ebon to another island, became attached to the missionaries, and spoke their praises at every island where they touched. The missionaries proceeded on their voyage to Kusaie, but with a deep conviction that the Lord was calling them back to the Marshall group.

At length (1857) the Morning Star, the children's vessel, heaves in sight at Kusaie. She brings Mr. and Mrs. Bingham, and Kanakaole with his wife, on their way to the Marshall and the Gilbert Islands. They are joined here by Messrs. Pierson and Doane, and sail for their destination. As they set out for Ebon Island, of the Marshall group, they are solemnly warned by old sea-captains of the danger that awaits them from that ferocious people. On approaching the island, the captain put up his boarding nettings, stationed his men fore and aft, and anxiously awaited the issue. Fifteen canoes drew near, jammed full of men. In the prow of the foremost stood a powerful man, with a wreath on his head and huge rings in his ears. On they came; but in the same instant Dr. Pierson and the savage recognized each other as old acquaintances, and the savage came on board shouting, " Docotor, docotor," in perfect delight. Many months before, it seems, this man and a hundred others had been driven by a storm upon Kusaie, where the missionaries had rescued them, and befriended them with food and medicine; and they had returned to their homes in peace. So the Lord befriended the missionaries in turn, and prepared them a welcome among the so-called " cannibals." And when, after a further cruise of thirty days, the Morning Star returned to leave the missionaries at Ebon, they were met on the water by twenty canoe loads of people, shouting, singing, and dancing for joy. On the shore they were received with every demonstration of friendship; and the aged female chief, who had once sailed with Dr. Pierson among the islands, took him by both hands and led him joyfully to her house. On the same voyage Mr. Bingham and Kanoa were set down at Apaiang, of the Gilbert group, where the king gave them a pleasant home.

Thus was the gospel first carried to these three groups of islands; and here we leave them, and their fellow-laborers that followed them, chiefly Hawaiians, at their self-denying toils. We will briefly sketch the progress of the work on the principal island, Ponape, as a specimen of the whole. Here the king, though almost helpless with the palsy, was friendly to the enterprise; while the Nanakin, his chief officer, expressed himself warmly, and received an English book with the avowed determination to learn to read it; " the cooper should teach him how, or he would pound him." Two short months sufficed to awaken the enmity of unprincipled foreigners. Two captains had bought one of the small islands, and made out a deed for the Nanakin to sign. He brought it to the missionaries, who found it to contain

the grossest frauds, including even the forgery of the Nanakin's sig-
nature.   The exposure of course created hostility.   Six months
brought fifteen vessels ; and though in most instances the captains
were friendly, and even kind, every arrival was attended with deplorable
influences on the morals of the native women.   Then came the opening of a school, some of the scholars sitting patiently for six long
hours to get an opportunity to steal.   Then came the small-pox ; and
before the end of the first year, it had carried off multitudes of the
inhabitants, broken up the school, arrested all plans of labor, pros-
trated the Hawaiian preacher, and produced a general recklessness
and bitterness of feeling through the island.   To add to the evil, the
vaccine matter received from the Sandwich Islands proved worthless ;
and wicked foreigners circulated the report that the missionaries had
introduced and were spreading the disease.   By resorting boldly to
inoculation, and beginning with the Nanakin, the missionaries at
length saved many lives and regained confidence.   In the midst of
this calamity, Mr. Sturges's house burned up, with all its contents,
driving him and his family to the woods.   Hostilities arose also among
the tribes, attended with robberies and murders ; and the sailors
continued to bring moral pollution.   One day, in his accustomed
tour, Mr. Sturges passed near three brothels, all kept by foreigners.
But the missionaries toiled on, resumed their schools, gathered their
growing congregations, privately sowed the good seed, and in four
years' time were printing hymns and Old Testament stories in Pona-
pean.   After a night of eight years, three converts were at one
time received to their little church, followed by eight others soon ;
and meanwhile a little church of six members was formed in another
part of the island.   Revivals brought opposition and more or less of
persecution.   At length a chapel is built in the mountains by native
hands, and at the principal station a church edifice, forty feet by sixty,
solemnly dedicated to God.   Hardly was it consecrated, when the
Morning Star arrived with an eight hundred pound bell, the gift of
friends in Illinois ; and within a fortnight the Nanakin, with his wife
and fourteen other converts, sat down at the table of the Lord.   The
chief had vibrated back and forth — now proclaiming Sabbath observance, breaking up five brothels, and following the missionary
round the island, and now distributing "toddy" profusely among
the people — till at length the Lord brought him in.   Half the
islanders had by this time yielded an outward deference to the true
religion.   Early in the year 1867, there were religious services regularly held at twelve principal places, a thousand readers, 161 church
members in good standing, and numbers of converts soon to be

received. Three new churches had been erected by the natives within two years, in one of which (in May, 1867) one hundred communicants sat down to the Lord's table in the presence of six hundred spectators, on the very spot where, fourteen years before, Mr. Sturges was near being overcome and robbed; and another of these churches, just built, though seating five hundred persons, will soon need to be enlarged. At Kusaie, there are 183 church members, of whom 93 were received in 1867. Three stone chapels had just been erected, four native deacons ordained, and the eye of the missionary turned to one man — the only living child of "good King George"— for a native pastor; while the influence of the churches is reacting on the sailors. There are about sixty church members now at the Marshall Islands, and the prospects are eminently hopeful. In the Gilbert group it is still seed-time, but the knowledge is spreading from island to island.

Among the laborers are ten Hawaiian missionaries, who have toiled wisely and faithfully. On many of these islands the population is steadily growing less. Possibly the religious books that now exist in these several tongues may one day lie, like Eliot's Indian Bible, without a reader; but they will be monuments of noble Christian self-denial, and mementoes of souls gathered into the kingdom of heaven.

The following persons have been sent from the United States to the Micronesia mission : —

| NAMES. | Sailed for the Mission. | Left or Released. | Died. |
|---|---|---|---|
| Rev. B. G. Snow. . . . . . | Nov. 18, 1851. | | |
| Mrs. Lydia V. Snow. . . . . . | " | | |
| Rev. L. H. Gulick. . . . . | " | | |
| Mrs. Louisa G. Gulick. . . . | " | | |
| Rev. A. A. Sturgess. . . . . | Jan. 17, 1852. | | . |
| Mrs. Susan. M. Sturgess. . . . | " | | |
| Rev. E. T. Doane. . . . . . | June 4, 1854. | | |
| Mrs. S. W. W. Doane.* . . . | " | | 1863 |
| Mrs. Clara C. Doane. . . . . | May, 1865. | | |
| Rev. Geo. Pierson, M. D. . . . | Nov. 28, 1854. | '59 or '60 | |
| Mrs. Nancy A. Pierson. . . . | " | " | |
| Rev. Hiram Bingham, Jr. . . . | Dec. 2, 1857. | | |
| Mrs. Minerva C. Bingham. . . . . | " | | |
| Rev. Eph. P. Roberts. . . . | June 24, 1858. | 1862 | |
| Mrs. Myra H. Roberts. . . . . | " | " | |

According to the latest statistics received, the church members, in regular standing, in Micronesia, were — on Ponape, 178; Kusaie, 179; Ebon, 80; Apaiang, 8. Total, 445; of whom 144 had been received within the last year. This number of church members, it is well said in a general letter from the mission, "does not indicate all that has been wrought by the saving power of the gospel."

# SKETCH OF THE MARQUESAS MISSION.

It remains to say a few words of the Marquesas. The mission here is in every aspect most remarkable, whether we consider the character of the people, the origin, the agency, or the influence of the mission. The Marquesas Islands, six in number, are situated nearly as far from Micronesia as from Hawaii. They are of volcanic formation, their mountains rising to the height of four or five thousand feet, with a wonderful grandeur and variety of scenery. The climate is fine, and the valleys unsurpassed in fertility, abounding in all manner of tropical fruits and vegetation. The fruits hang temptingly upon the trees, or drop on the ground. The islands contain about 8,000 people, of Malay origin, speaking a language very similar to the Hawaiian. The natives have fine athletic forms, great vivacity and quick apprehension, but are to the last degree impatient of labor and control. They are, in fact, among the most lawless, quarrelsome, and ferocious of the tribes of men. They have no acknowledged form of government. The individual gluts his revenge unhindered; and the clans in the various valleys are in perpetual warfare. The bodies of the slain are cut in pieces, and distributed among the clan to be devoured, the little children even partaking of the horrid meal. In 1859, when the whale-ship Tarlight was wrecked off the island of Hivaoa, the natives conspired to massacre the crew in order to plunder the vessel — though in both objects they were frustrated. The community cannot have forgotten the letter of President Lincoln to the missionary Kekela, a few years ago, thanking him for his services in rescuing the mate of an American ship, Mr. Whalon, from being roasted and eaten by these cannibals. The disposition of the natives is to some degree symbolized by their personal appearance — the men hideously tattooed with lizards, snakes, birds, and fishes, and the women smeared with cocoanut oil and turmeric. Add to this the

(30)

most oppressive system of tabus, so that, for example, the father, the mother, and the grown-up daughter must all eat apart from each other, and we have some idea of the obstacles to the Christian religion in those islands.

Some years ago, a Hawaiian youth was left by a vessel at these islands, sick. He recovered, and by his superior knowledge became a man of importance, and married the daughter of the High Chief, Mattunui. The father-in-law was so impressed with his acquisitions, which, as he learned, were derived from the missionaries, that after consultation with the other chiefs, he embarked for Lahaina, to seek missionaries for Marquesas. This was in 1853. The Hawaiian Society felt that the call was from God. Two native pastors — one of them Kekela — and two native teachers, accompanied by their wives, were deputed to go. They were welcomed with joy. Mattunui sat up all night to tell of the " strange things " he saw and heard in the Hawaiian Islands ; and an audience of a hundred and fifty listened to preaching on the following Sabbath. The missionaries entered at once on their various forms of Christian activity, organizing their schools, and in due time translating the Gospel of John. One foreigner alone was with them, — Mr. Bicknell, an English mechanic, a noble man, afterwards ordained a preacher ; otherwise the whole enterprise was Hawaiian. Roman Catholic priests hurried at once to the islands, but the Hawaiian preachers held on, amid immense discouragements, with great energy and perseverance, and with admirable good sense. At length God gave them the first convert, Abraham Natua. Soon after this the missionaries determined to break down the system of tabus, and a great feast was gotten up on the mission premises, at which the High Chief, Mattunui, and many others, sat down for the first time with their wives, and broke through the system in every available direction. It was a grand blow at the whole institution. In four years the intolerable thievishness of the natives was so far checked within the range of the missions, that clothing could be exposed and the mission premises could be left unlocked the entire day, with perfect safety. Urgent calls came from various parts of the islands for missionaries — five or six pieces of land, more than could be occupied, being given in Hivaoa alone. Converts came dropping in slowly, one by one at first ; and a quiet and powerful influence has been diffusing itself through the islands, and filling the minds of these devoted preachers with great hopes of the future. In 1867 there were eleven male and female missionaries at the island, who had organized five churches with fifty-seven members, and were about to establish a boarding school for boys and another for girls. And in 1868 Mr. Coan, who had just visited the islands, wrote thus: " The light and love and gravitating power of the gospel are permeating the dead masses of the Marquesans. Scores already appear as true disciples of Jesus. Scores can read the word of the living God, and it is a power within them. Hundreds have forsaken the tabus, and hundreds of others hold them lightly. Consistent missionaries and their teachings are respected. Their lives and persons are sacred where human life is no more regarded than that of a dog. They go secure where others dare not go. They leave houses, wives, and children without fear, and savages protect them. Everywhere we see evidence of the silent and sure progress of truth, and we rest assured that the time to favor the dark Marquesans has come." Whether we view the people on whom or the people by whom this power has been put forth, we see alike a signal movement of the gospel of Christ.

# DR. ANDERSON'S WORK ON THE HAWAIIAN ISLANDS.

BY ANDREW P. PEABODY, D.D., CAMBRIDGE, MASS.

[From the Boston Review for May, 1865.]

*The Hawaiian Islands: Their Progress and Condition under Missionary Labors.* By RUFUS ANDERSON, D.D., Foreign Secretary of the American Board of Commissioners for Foreign Missions. With Illustrations. Boston : Gould & Lincoln. 1864.

WE may profess implicit faith in the geological theories which adequately account for the condition and contents of the earth's crust ; yet our faith in them lacks vividness, simply because no one of the world-forming processes has taken place under our own observation, or under the eye of witnesses who have told us their story. But were there at this moment an unfinished continent or island, still the abode of Saurian reptiles, or the laboratory of fossil coal, the fresh record of explorations in that region would convert our cosmogony from a vague or dead belief into a clearly conceived and intensely realized system of nature.

There has been in the remote past a social, there has been a religious cosmogony, and the greatest difficulty in the way of correct apprehensions as to the origin of civilization, and as to the methods of growth in the primitive church, lies in our lack of realizing and satisfying conceptions of the elements involved in each separate problem. The history of civilization is wrapped in obscurity. The veil of the Dark Ages fell upon certain savage tribes that had the mastery of Europe ; it rose upon those tribes, still, indeed, rude in many of the arts of life, but already in an advanced condition of culture and of potential refinement. When we go back to the earlier civilization, we are equally unable to ascend to its cradle and to define the first stages of its growth. Yet birth and source it must have had, heavenly or earthly, and we all have our theories of its genesis ;

1

but we hold them loosely and impassively, because it is so utterly impossible for us to conceive of the transmutation of savage into civilized man. Thus also, there was a creative era of the Christian church, a period when the transition was made, often simultaneously by large numbers of men and women, from Paganism or from Jewish ritualism to a vital faith in the Gospel. Of this era we have numerous memorials in the New Testament. The Epistles are full of the controversies, cases of conscience, weaknesses, scandals, causes of apostasy, incident to this infantile condition. But, though we doubt not the inspiration of the sacred writers, we are apt to enter with but feeble appreciation into the details of their casuistry; many of the topics which they treat seriously seem to us too trivial for grave animadversion; and in not a few cases they recognize as perfectly consistent with a position in the church states of character and modes of conduct which we should regard as incompatible with the Christian name. We thus find it hard to conceive of the earlier portions of Christian history, and while we devoutly acknowledge in them the divine working, we fail to discern the phases of humanity which the record simply describes without interpreting them. But if, after an interval of many centuries, these primitive civilizing and Christianizing processes have been renewed in our own time, even on a comparatively small scale; if even in the least of the nations an organic revolution such as had passed out of human expectation is now nearly consummated, the spectacle has a profound interest equally for the student of history and for the expositor of the Sacred Word.

Such a spectacle is exhibited in the book before us. On merely philosophical grounds it is of unique value. It shows us the means and steps of civilization, the circumstances which favor or check its growth, the action upon it of ideas and institutions respectively, its relations of cause and effect to religious culture. It throws essential light on even the most recondite questions, such as that of the possibility of a nation's becoming civilized except by aid or influence from without, that of man's primitive condition upon the earth, that of his decline or progress from his first estate.

Equally instructive, as we hope to show in the sequel, will this book be found by the biblical scholar. Since reading it, we have understood the Epistles to the Corinthians better than ever before, and have been led, as by no merely critical study, to admire the prudence, sagacity, insight and foresight of the inspired author, no less than his tender forbearance and charity for the newly converted under their liability to the trail and soil of the worship they had abjured. At the same time, we have here full verification of the aggressive power of Christianity in circumstances in no wise favorable for its reception. We learn that it was not as the outgrowth of its own age that the Gospel found reception when first promulgated, but that it is the everlasting Gospel, endowed with like life-giving energy for all times and nations. We especially prize this testimony at a period when naturalism is attempting to sap the foundations of our faith. Other religions have shown themselves the congenial products of their own birthtime by the failure of all attempts to extend their empire, otherwise than by force, in subsequent generations. They grow for a while, rapidly it may be, because they embody and sanction ideas level with the culture of their age ; but as the race advances, or changes without advancing, they have no hold, except on the populations which they have educated, and cramped and dwarfed in educating them. A divinely given religion alone can be free from these limitations of time and race, and can work in the eternal freshness of its power on minds of every grade and of every form of culture.

But, most of all, as lovers of mankind, do we rejoice in the evidence here given of a new Pentecost of Christian salvation, in the assurance of the birth into the eternal life of thousands of perishing souls, in the establishment of the reign of Christ upon the ruins of savage fetichism, in the songs of Zion that have replaced the cannibal's war-whoop, in the altars of redemption railed with the broken spears of fierce idolators, in the homes that from beastly dens have become nurseries for heaven.

We should incur the charge of extravagance were we to attempt to convey the impression made upon us by Dr. Anderson's book. His tour among the Hawaiian Islands seems to us the most magnificent progress recorded in history ; and his simple, modest narrative, so entirely devoid of egotism and of exaggeration, only makes us feel the more profoundly the greatness of his mission and the preëminent fitness of the agent. Dr.

Anderson in his youth devoted himself in purpose to the career of a foreign missionary, and from the time when he first found the Gospel precious to his own soul, the needs and claims of the unevangelized have never been absent from his thought. In the pendency of arrangements for an Eastern mission, he accepted a temporary clerical appointment on the staff of the American Board. This appointment was soon made permanent; after eight years of service as Assistant Secretary, on the death of Rev. Dr. Cornelius, in 1832, he became one of the three Corresponding Secretaries; and for nearly thirty years he has held the first place in the administration of that noble charity. It is not easy to tell what fertility of resource, what sagacity in the discernment of character, what world-wide knowledge, what executive ability, what hold upon the confidence of good men in all lands, what extended power of influence, have been needed and developed in a life like his. On his prudence, patience, judgment, energy, the entire system has depended, to a degree most fully appreciated by those who have been most intimately conversant with his labors. No statesman or diplomatist has held in his hands so many threads of affairs, often delicate and complicated, often of decisive moment, often involving even grave national interests, demanding with the directness and integrity that befit the servant of the Most High a fully equal measure of the subtile skill and adroit management, in which the children of this world are so apt to surpass the children of the light, and for lack of which a large portion of the philanthropy which has the purest record in heaven leaves no enduring traces of itself on earth.

When Dr. Anderson entered on his official duties, the second instalment of missionaries to the Hawaiian Islands had been despatched, many of the natives were under hopeful training, the language had been reduced to its alphabetic elements, and the first essays at printing had been successfully made. But at that time the mission was a still doubtful experiment. Shortly afterward, the regent, and nine of the principal chiefs were gathered into the Christian church, vast multitudes were awakened to a lively interest in the Gospel, and the transformation of institutions, habits, domestic and social life took place so rapidly as to leave no longer room for fear of the reëstablishment of idolatry. During Dr. Anderson's secretaryship more than a hundred missionaries, clerical and lay, male and female, have been sent to the Islands from the United States, under his instruction and direction, while to the Home Board have been constantly referred vital questions of policy and administration, both civil and ecclesiastical, involving difficult relations with the emissaries and officers of foreign governments, and with missionaries, sometimes intrusive, from other religious bodies. Less than the soundest discretion, the most determined vigor, and the most watchful and persistent assiduity on the part of the American Board would at various crises of the mission have placed its interests at fearful hazard, and occasioned disastrous decline in the religious condition of the natives.

In 1862, the Hawaiian people was deemed to hold its rightful place among Christian nations, and the question was raised as to the gradual withdrawal of the support of the Board, with the view of leaving the Islands to support their own religious institutions, and to furnish their own Christian teachers. To ascertain data for the safe and judicious settlement of this question it was thought desirable to send an officer of the Board to the Islands, and especially fitting was it to delegate this commission to him who had for nearly forty years identified himself with the work, and who could claim as his "children in the Lord" those thousands of redeemed and converted savages. It was for him an antepast of the blessedness of heaven. Seldom can he who sows in tears count on earth his ranks of ripened sheaves. Even in the ordinary Christian ministry, while the faithful servant of Christ is never without ground for encouragement and gratitude, a collective view of vast results is not often vouchsafed to him; and many there are who have effected so little to the outward eye compared with their longing and endeavor, that they go to their rest feeling that much of their strength has been spent for naught, and only in the day when the secrets of all hearts shall be revealed, will they know their share in the harvest-work. But as Dr. Anderson passed from village to village and from island to island, he was permitted to see in great part the accumulated fruits of his life-toil, multiplied tokens of a regeneration in which his had been the controlling mind, evidences of a work of grace in which he had been the favored instrument, whose magnitude is to be estimated not by past and present converts, but by the unborn multitudes that shall enter on their Christian heritage. He was everywhere received with the love and reverence due to a father in Christ; thanks to God for his visit were sung in that language so strange to his ear; his advent was rapturously welcomed by immense congregations of the natives; he united in the celebration of the Saviour's death, with larger bodies of believers than he can often meet in his own land; his words of faith and love, interpreted by his missionary brethren, were listened to with intense earnestness, and met with the most fervent response; and liberal contributions for the distribution of the Scriptures and the furtherance of the Gospel were pressed upon him by those so recently brought from darkness into God's marvellous light. It was, indeed, a triumphal march through this newly conquered province of the Redeemer's empire—how unspeakably blessed to one who felt so profoundly that in all these offerings of affection, gratitude and veneration he was but receiving tribute for the King of kings!

Trusting that most of our readers have sought or will seek for themselves the instruction and edification proffered by the book before us, we shall enter into none of the details of Dr. Anderson's journeyings and personal experiences, but shall confine ourselves to a brief sketch of the former and present condition of the Hawaiian people, and a discussion of a few of the many subjects of interest treated or suggested by the author.

The Hawaiian Islands are ten in number. The native inhabitants bear in color, features and language strong affinities to the Malays, from whom they were probably derived. The population, at the arrival of the first missionaries, was estimated at one hundred and thirty five thousand, that of Hawaii, the principal island, at eighty thousand. The people were in the lowest condition of savage life. Their genial climate and spontaneously fertile soil had precluded the development of even the rude arts, of which in higher latitudes necessity would have been the teacher. Their dwellings were utterly devoid of comfort; their clothing insufficient for decency. The rights of property were hardly recognized. Extortion on the part of the chiefs, mutual theft and robbery among the people, seem to have been the common law. Polygamy was habitual among all who could obtain and support a plurality of wives, and licentiousness prevailed to the very verge of promiscuous concubinage. Infanticide was so prevalent as to have led to a marked decline of the population, two thirds of the children that were born having been buried barely to avoid the trouble of bringing them up. Murders and crimes of violence were perpetrated almost without restraint; and human sacrifices were offered for the recovery of the king when sick, and as victims at his obsequies. The natural conscience seems to have been obliterated, and there was no trace of a recognized distinction between right and wrong.

The prevalent idolatry was of the coarsest and most senseless type, consisting in the worship of hideous images, with no idea even of their being symbols of unseen powers. This idolatry was extirpated, by a unique combination of circumstances, about the time of the embarkation of the first American missionaries. It was a case in which Satan successfully cast out Satan, through the mysterious working of Him who makes even the wrath and guilt of man to praise him. Among the superstitions inseparable from the national religion was a stringent *tabu* system, extending not only to sacred days, places and persons, but to the domestic habits. Women were forbidden to eat in the presence of their husbands, and were debarred from many of the choicest articles of diet, whether fruit, flesh or fish. The violation of these interdicts was punishable by death, and it was supposed that the offender who escaped human vengeance would be destroyed by the gods. Foreigners had introduced ardent spirits, and to all the other sins of this degraded race was now superadded the habit of beastly drunkenness. The female chiefs, when intoxicated, found courage to indulge in prohibited food. Their rank secured them from punishment at the hand of man, and they were not slow in discovering that no vindictive bolt was launched at their heads by the divinity they had outraged. This *tabu* system seems to have been the fundamental doctrine, the *articulus stantis vel cadentis ecclesiæ* of their creed, and, this proved false, they found themselves atheists. The destruction of their idols, the burning of their temples ensued; and the missionaries discovered, for the first time in the world, an utterly godless people.

It can not be denied that this condition of things offered a vantage-ground for the labors of the earliest Christian teachers, yet less than might seem at first thought. Had the people been far enough advanced in spiritual development to feel the need of worship or to crave objects of reverence, the *rasa tabula* thus presented would have been easily written over with the holy names of the Christian faith. But these conditions precedent of religious belief seem to have been wanting. The tablet was not there. Yet undoubtedly it was easier, humanly speaking, to create it, than it would have been to make a palimpsest. The resistance presented by the *vis inertiæ* of a race utterly *dead* in trespasses and sins was less than might have been opposed by vital and vigorous misbelief. The seeds of faith lie in the depraved heart, and the dew of the divine grace which alone can make them fruitful is seldom wanting to fervent prayer and faithful endeavor. But, this one feature excepted, the condition of the Hawaiians in 1820 presented as unpromising a field for evangelic culture as lay anywhere beneath the sun, and, compared with the primitive age of the church, an immeasurably less hopeful field than any of the communities to which the apostles carried the word of life.

What are they now? In the arts of civilized life their progress has been at least equal to their conscious needs. While the chiefs and many of the inhabitants of the towns have well-built and well-furnished houses, the squalidness and misery of the rural districts and the poorer classes have given place to habits of decency and self-respect. The government has a written Constitution, with a Bill of Rights as liberal as that of Massachusetts, and with the powers of king, legislature and judiciary carefully defined and limited. The laws are wise, equitable, and preëminently Christian, guarding the religious liberty of the people, but providing against the desecration of the Sabbath and against the renewal of idolatrous superstitions and observances. The courts are admirably organized, and the judicial offices filled by men of competent ability and proved integrity, in part by native citizens, one of the three judges of the Supreme Court being a Hawaiian. There is no country in Christendom, in which life and property are more secure, and none in which the laws against intemperance and licentiousness are more vigilantly and rigidly executed. In the native language there have been published twenty thousand copies of the entire Bible, twelve thousand of the New Testament, and more than two hundred works beside, including school-books, books of religious instruction, and general literature. Three Hawaiian newspapers are issued. The Report of 1849 gives two hundred and eighty nine schools, with eight thousand six hundred and twenty eight scholars. There are several boarding schools, both for boys and girls, at which a superior education is afforded, and a High School, which would bear comparison with our best New England academies, and which has graduated nearly eight hundred pupils, ten of whom have been ordained as ministers of the Gospel. Algebra, Geometry, Trigonometry, Surveying and Political Economy are among the higher branches of learning which have been successfully taught. The people manifest a singular aptness for the acquisition of knowledge, and display an equal susceptibility for the ideas, impressions, tastes and habits which belong of right to advancing intellectual culture.

We can not need to say that this social renovation has been, not only coincident with and incidental to, but commensurate with and dependent upon, the action of Christian truth on individual hearts, and through them on the great heart of the nation. The history of that people for the last forty years has been a multiform commentary on the text: "The entrance of Thy word giveth light." As regards domestic and social habits, we have no evidence that the missionaries have busied themselves especially in the details of improvement. But the Christian consciousness is quick and keen in detecting incongruities and improprieties; the æsthetic nature is stimulated, nourished and instructed by the Divine Spirit, which is the Spirit of beauty no less than of grace; and the consecration of the body and all that pertains to the outward life, by purity, decency, neatness and order, can hardly fail to accompany or follow the consecration of the soul to the service of God. This exterior reformation must needs bear a close proportion, in its extent and thoroughness, to the energy of the work of grace. In these Islands the Gospel had from the first free course among the chiefs and the men and women of commanding influence, and its power was early felt through the whole people. In 1838 there was a great awakening throughout the entire nation, which resulted in the accession of many thousands of genuine converts to the churches. In 1843 more than a fourth part of the entire population were professing Christians; a larger proportion, it is believed, than could be found anywhere else in Christendom. To all these the missionary stations were centres of light, places of familiar resort, seminaries for instruction in things secular no less than in things spiritual. The superior fitness of the habits and appliances of civilized life was promptly perceived and felt; and the disciples, of necessity, became imitators of the teachers and their families in such portions of their mode of living as were applicable to their own condition. This last limitation is essential to a just estimate of the degree of their civilization. Had the missionaries themselves, with all their culture and refinement, belonged to a race for many generations domesticated in that climate, their artificial wants would have been much fewer and more simple; and it would seem to be the tendency of the great mass of their converts to adopt from them just such improvements as they need for decency and comfort, while those who from their position in the state are brought into more intimate relations with the foreign residents conform more fully to foreign tastes and habits. With this essential qualification the Hawaiians already merit a place among civilized nations — a much higher place than would be accorded to the Greeks with their glorious heritage and their little more than nominal Christianity; and they hold this position solely through the transforming power of religious faith and culture.

It is, also, because they have so readily received the divine word, that they have become to so extraordinary a degree an educated and a reading people. The Bible enlarges the mental horizon, suggests themes of thought, subjects of inquiry, gives a sacredness and a zest to knowledge of every kind, stimulates study, and generates mental activity. There evidently exists in this so lately benighted community a higher type of intellectual life, a more genuine love of learning, a surer promise of advanced and extended culture, than can be found in the mass of any people in Europe or America which is debarred free access to the oracles of divine truth.

As for the actual religious condition of these Islands, we have spoken of the proportion of church members in 1843. It is nearly or quite as large at the present time. In the judgment of Dr. Anderson and other equally intelligent witnesses, the evidences of sincere piety are as general and as satisfactory as among professed believers in any portion of Christendom.

## 11

Family prayer is almost universal among the converts. The Sabbath is kept sacred to an unusual degree, and its worship is attended by numerous, in some places, by vast congregations. Social prayer meetings are established in connection with every church, and are maintained with constancy, and often with zeal. The average moral character of the church-members is in most respects high, even by the standard of our older civilization, and the sins which have led to frequent ecclesiastical censure and excommunication, though more patent to rebuke, are certainly no more inconsistent with the spirit of our religion than the worldliness, penuriousness and meanness which pass unchallenged among the guests at our communion tables. Indeed, what indicates, perhaps, more clearly than all things else, the prevalent sincerity of these islanders is their readiness to give largely from their scanty means for the support and propagation of the Gospel. Their contributions average more than twenty thousand dollars annually, and their time and labor are always at the disposal of their teachers for the service of religion. In fine, though they not unfrequently show their still infantile estate as Christians, they at the same time exhibit abundant proof that the religion of the Gospel has wrought in thousands of hearts its regenerating work, and has so far leavened the entire community that there is no ground for apprehending a general apostasy or permanent decline.

We have dwelt on the evidences of their civilization, mainly with reference to the question which it was Dr. Anderson's special purpose to investigate, namely, the expediency of treating them as an integral part of Christendom, and gradually withdrawing from them the special tutelage of the Missionary Board. Their higher or lower degree of civilization or culture may not affect their present condition as Christians ; but in their capacity to transmit that condition it is a vital element. The soul of the rudest savage may be converted to God and prepared for heaven ; but the light that is in him can shed very little radiance around him. Christian institutions alone can perpetuate the power of the Gospel ; and they can be sustained and extended among a population of unsettled habits and undeveloped intellect, only through the agency of a superior race. At most of our flourishing missionary stations the withdrawal of the missionaries would be followed by the speedy extinction of

all Christian life. A self-perpetuating church implies the establishment of permanent homes and regular modes of industry, a
forethought adequate to provide for future exigencies, mutual
confidence among fellow-worshippers, the capacity of combined
and organized action, and the existence of means of education,
and habits of mental industry sufficient to ensure a well-trained
ministry and a supply of intelligent office-bearers and leaders
in church affairs. A community of which all this could be af-
firmed is to all intents and purposes civilized, and has within itself
resources for further advancement and higher attainment. And
in this sense the Hawaiians are civilized. We care not whether
they live in houses of grass or of stone, sleep on mats or beds,
sit on the ground or on chairs, eat with their fingers or with
forks. These matters have no concern with civilization, that is,
with the culture which fits men to be citizens and fellow-citizens.

Christianity always tends to civilize a community; but in order to produce this result, it must establish its control over the
ruling classes, must permeate the body politic, mould its
institutions, preside over its legislation, govern its social intercourse, and, above all, give character to the relations
between husband and wife, parent and child, master and servant. Where this work has been in a good measure accomplished, its consummation may be retarded by the prolonga-
tion of foreign influence, however beneficent. It is well
neither for individual nor collective humanity to remain in tutelage when the period of maturity has been reached. Guard-
ianship beyond its due term cripples and dwarfs the faculties
of self-help which it has created. We must, therefore, acknowledge the wisdom of the action of the American Board,
in relinquishing the immediate control of the religious interests
of these Islands to their native and resident population. The
Board still provides for the maintenance of the missionaries
already established, most of whom have passed the prime of
active usefulness. The counsel and influence of these tried,
approved and trusted teachers will be of essential benefit in
the transition from pupilage to self-government, while the
churches, unburthened by the necessity of contributing to their
support, will have no obstacle in the way of securing and com-
pensating the services of native ministers. At the same time
those recent heathen are encouraged themselves to enter on the

field of missionary enterprise, and this most wisely ; for among the means of grace giving is second only to prayer, as the American church has found in its own blessed experience. The superintendence of the Micronesian mission is to be entrusted to an executive board chosen by the Hawaiian Evangelical Association, the American Board continuing its pecuniary aid for such time and in such measure as may be found necessary.

We have thus far presented only the bright and hopeful aspects of the Christian cause on these Islands. Is there not a reverse side? That there is we could not doubt, even were our author silent with regard to it. But, with his perfect candor, Dr. Anderson suppresses nothing, and our readers will miss in his pages not one of the salient facts which have been employed with malign purpose and effect by the calumniators of the mission. We have not referred to these facts in discussing the self-sustaining capacity of the Hawaiian churches, because they are not of sufficient magnitude to have any important bearing on that question, any more than the short-comings, dissensions and corruptions of our New England Christianity have on its power to prolong its own existence, and, by aid from on high, to purify and elevate its own standard of faith and piety. But we will now look at the shades in the picture.

In the first place, it must be admitted that there remains among the Hawaiian Christians a certain proclivity to licentiousness and intemperance. We are grieved, but not surprised or shocked at this. It is what is to be expected in a people separated by hardly a generation from an utterly brutish state of manners and morals. Aside from the theological question of original sin, though casting essential light upon it, there can be no doubt as to the transmission of moral tendencies in families and races. Had one of Herod's children become a disciple of Christ, he would have been a disciple of a very different type from one of the family of Joseph of Arimathea. He might repeatedly, under stress of sudden and intense temptation, have shown his sonship according to the flesh to the vilest of men, yet without losing from his heart the evidence of his spiritual sonship. Just such is the case with a tribe or race of converts from the lower forms of paganism. There is a heritage of evil in their very constitution of body, mind and soul. Ages of slavery to the animal appetites have stimulated those appetites, and given them a natively larger influence over the active powers of the moral nature than they have in a people whose nature has been moulded by centuries of self-control and mental and religious culture. The Christian consciousness may be as genuine and as strong in the recent savage as in the descendant from an ancestry of saints; yet in the former case it will have to contend with a host of the powers of evil, which in the latter were resisted and overcome in the remote past, and have since fought only with blunted weapons and with crippled strength. It must be remembered, too, that the social sentiments and habits of decency and propriety, which are a most essential safeguard and help to the individual Christian, at least in the early stages of the religious life, are of gradual growth and of cumulative efficacy, and that they have but just begun to grow in the Hawaiian people. It is said by the Spirit of God to every subject of renewing grace, as it was said to Abraham, "Get thee out of thine own country, and from thy kindred, and thy father's house, unto a land that I will show thee"; and the reality, intensity and working power of his faith are to be tested, not by the distance yet to be measured to the promised land, but by his distance from his starting point. He who moves on his pilgrimage from an idolatrous country, from kindred steeped in swinish sensuality, from a father's house no better than a kennel, may find himself at the close of a long and faithful pilgrimage below the starting point of natural conscience and conventional morality, at which the child of a consecrated household hears and obeys the same call of God; yet in the eye of heaven he will have fought a good fight, and have finished a noble course, and his children may commence where he closed his career.

As we have intimated, the details in the volume before us at once receive light from, and reflect light upon, the apostolic epistles. In the churches at Corinth and in Asia, St. Paul certainly recognizes as brethren beloved, and praises for their proficiency and good gifts as Christians, persons who needed advice and warning as to the very rudiments of morality. At Corinth there had been gross violations of chastity among the disciples, and it would seem that even the Lord's Supper had been made an occasion of excess and drunkenness. In fine, there was in that church a condition of things incompatible, according to our modern notions, with the lowest concrete form of vital Christianity. Yet in his second epistle we discern manifest traces in these frail novices of a sensitiveness to rebuke, an accessibleness to the movements of contrite sorrow, indicating all that is implied in the apostle's words as to the depth of Christian feeling in their hearts and the reality of their conversion to God. "For behold this self-same thing, that ye sorrowed after a godly sort, what carefulness it wrought in you, yea, what clearing of yourselves, yea, what indignation, yea, what fear, yea, what vehement desire, yea, what zeal"! St. Paul, it must be borne in mind, in view of these moral infirmities of his converts, is slow to condemn, chary of excommunication, prompt and earnest in the restoration of offenders, aware all the while that, though "the iniquity of their heels" — the sins in which they were born and bred, yet which they have in purpose left behind them — may at times "compass them about," there may yet be on their hearts the unobliterated seal of the Spirit. We can not but agree with some of the missionaries, as cited by Dr. Anderson, that among these modern converts excommunication has been too frequent, especially as the excommunicated have in numerous instances passed from a church which would have tolerated, not their sin, but their bitterly repented sin, to the less discriminating mercies of Romanism, which, whatever may be its theories, practically makes the way of transgressors easy.

The same sensitiveness to rebuke, which St. Paul recognizes among the Corinthians, may be remarked among the Hawaiians. Says Dr. Anderson, "I was assured of cases where, after a terrible declension, the return had been with increased humility, experience, watchfulness, and zeal, so that the lapsed recovered ones became at length pillars in the church."

So far from looking upon lapses of this kind, though frequent, as a ground of discouragement, we rather regard them, viewed in all their aspects, as a hopeful omen. It is an immense gain that the community has reached a condition in which such cases of sin are exceptional and abnormal, are not numerous enough to constitute a characteristic feature of the Christian society or to defy its discipline, and are already the objects of unfeigned shame and contrition among the guilty, and of hearty reprobation among their associates. Moreover, this unfortunate liability, so far as it exists, seems to be confined chiefly to those who have been heathen and savages, and is not likely to be transmitted to their children except in a modified and controllable form and degree. The now rising generation, trained under the shadow of the domestic altar and the Christian sanctuary, educated by religious teachers, imbued from their tender years in the morality of the Gospel, and large numbers of them made in their youth hopeful subjects of Divine grace, will grow up under at least as favorable influences as those which surround the young persons in our own land whom we regard as the hope of the church. This future is already beginning to be realized. The pupils of the missionary schools are fast establishing a higher tone of character. Of the native ministers we are told that not one has shown himself unworthy of his sacred trust. The manifest tendency is toward an elevated standard of practical ethics.

In this connection we can not but attach great importance to the laws of the kingdom, not only or chiefly in their prohibitory or punitive function, but as declarative of the collective moral sense, and as educating the general conscience. From all that we can learn, we infer that in the legislation, and at the hands of the judiciary of the Islands, purity and temperance are as carefully guarded as they can be by human authority, and that those who violate them can be protected only by the secrecy of their guilt. The laws against the manufacture of intoxicating drinks and against their sale to native residents are peculiarly stringent and severe, and a very recent attempt to relax the penalty for their sale has been defeated by the vote of nearly three fourths of the legislature — a vote which, as passed after able and thorough discussion, we feel warranted in regarding as an authentic exponent of public opinion.

Does it not appear from these statements that the easily besetting sins of the Hawaiians are treated with greater severity and present better promise of their rapid decline, than the vices that infect the religious communities of older Christendom — the selfishness, avarice and virtual dishonesty, which are "the abomination of desolation" in the church of God, and hold in sordid slavery many who claim to be its very pillars?

A much more serious discouragement to missionary labor on this field might seem to be found in the decline of the native population. On this subject it is not easy to obtain trustworthy data, either as to the extent to which causes of depopulation have operated in former times, or as to the degree in which they are now arrested. Captain Cook estimated the population at four hundred thousand; but this was undoubtedly an over-estimate. The earliest official census, in 1832, gives one hundred and thirty thousand, three hundred and fifteen; the latest, in 1860, sixty nine thousand, eight hundred. But for the first four years of these twenty eight, the decrease was at the rate of more than four per cent. per annum, while for the last seven years it has been less than two thirds of one per cent. per annum. The vices introduced by foreigners held a prominent place among the causes of the rapid decline from the first discovery of the Islands till the arrival of the missionaries. The passion for strong drink made fearful ravages among the people; while the vile lusts of their visitors from civilized lands brought upon them even still more loathsome agencies of disease and death, and undoubtedly weakened the vital stamina of coming generations. There has been also at three different periods since the commencement of the century a visitation of devastating epidemics, though it would seem that the liability to diseases of this class is much less than in regions not lying under the salubrious influence of breezes from the sea. Infanticide and human sacrifices must also account in part for the diminished numbers of the people, and the former of these causes must have very gradually ceased with the progress of Christianity. Then too, though the rude and squalid habits of savage life are not incompatible with a moderate growth of population, improvements in dwellings, dress, and medical treatment can hardly fail to preserve many lives that would else have been sacrificed in infancy, by needless exposure, or by curable disease. On the whole, we can not but believe that future enumerations will present results of a much more favorable character than the past, and that through the blessing of Providence this mild, gentle, tractable and highly improvable people may maintain its name and place among the nations of the earth, as a monument of Christian philanthropy, as a luculent token of the fulfilment of the promises of God, and as a centre and source of light to populations on the islands and coasts of the Pacific still lying under the shadow of death.

But were the case otherwise, were the gradual extinction of

this people clearly foreseen, would there be any the less reason to rejoice in what has been accomplished, and to extend to the declining remnant of the nation all the offices of Christian love? The salvation of thousands upon thousands of souls will still have rewarded the toil and sacrifice of the church and its agents; the national decline will have been retarded by this ministry of mercy; and there will have been written a chapter of the world's religious history, which we believe will be transcribed in letters of light in the Lamb's book of life.

We refer to this last named contingency, not because we think it probable, but because it may present itself to some of our readers as inevitable. It is undoubtedly a beneficent law of the divine Providence that races of feeble vitality and capacity shall yield place by the operation of natural causes to races of superior physical and intellectual vigor; in fine, that the different regions of the earth shall gradually pass into hands that can subdue it, avail themselves of its resources and enjoy its uses. Under this law, no doubt, the aborigines of North America will ultimately disappear, and the humane policy which ought to have been pursued to them from the first would not have ensured their preservation in the land, though it would have averted the condemnation of blood-guiltiness from the European settlers. But the Hawaiians do not seem to fall necessarily under this law. Their constitution is adapted to their climate; their capacity to their soil. They are amply able to develop the resources of their territory, and to employ for the general benefit the advantages of their position. They thus far show themselves susceptible of cultivation, and have made more rapid progress than has elsewhere left its record in the history of the world. They may not, indeed, have within themselves the elements of a great people; but their cluster of islets can never become the seat of a great people. They could not, indeed, protect themselves by arms against any of the leading powers of Christendom; but we trust that they will guard their modest independence by the arts and virtues that belong to a Christian nation, and by pacific and beneficent relations of intercourse and commerce. Their insular and solitary position may save them from dangerous complications with more powerful states; they can not lie on the track of any future belligerents, or become the victims of wars other than their own; and the time has gone by for aggression or usurpation from abroad, without shadow of reason or pretence of right.

Another danger to which this people is exposed grows out of the influx of foreign residents. Much of the land is peculiarly adapted to the growth of the sugar-cane, while rice, coffee and cotton are successfully cultivated. These commodities are most profitably raised on large plantations, and the soil suited to their production is already furnishing a lucrative investment for the disposable capital of France, England and America; while the commerce of the Islands has of necessity been hitherto conducted to a very great degree by immigrants from the older commercial nations. To these dominant classes of foreigners there have been recently added importations of coolies from China for labor on the sugar-plantations. If enterprise on the one hand and manual labor on the other are to be permanently usurped by immigrants, of course under this double pressure the native population will inevitably decline in resources and in energy, and will be gradually absorbed and obliterated by intermarriage with the intrusive races. But whether this shall be the case or not must depend, we believe, on the thoroughness of the civilizing and Christianizing work which has been wrought upon the natives. If considerable numbers of them are fitted in intelligence and character to hold commanding positions, and to conduct extended operations in agriculture and commerce, they will in the lapse of one or two generations replace the foreign residents; for, with equal ability, they will have the advantage in physical constitution, in attachment to the soil, in the command of the language, and in the confidence of their fellow-countrymen. If, at the other extremity of the social scale, Christian culture develops habits of industry and creates a felt need of the comforts of civilized life, the mass of the people will not suffer the soil to be cultivated by strangers.

The labor of coolies, while on moral grounds little preferable to that of slaves, is not much less costly and wasteful, their nominally low wages being hardly an offset to the expense of importation and the rapid mortality among them; and the Hawaiians, once made aware of the duty and the privilege of toil, will readily demonstrate the superior economy of free labor. Much of the land planted with sugar-cane is now in the hands of small native proprietors; and on these estates free labor is proved to be amply remunerative. On the whole we can not believe that a people that deserves to live can be pressed down and crushed out on its own soil. Foreign enterprise has gained its ascendancy, and foreign labor its foothold in the Hawaiian Islands, only while the natives are in training to take effective possession of their birthright. If they show themselves mentally or morally unfit to retain the heritage, we doubt not that Providence will bestow it on races more worthy of it. But in what God has done for this people, while we may not presume to lift the veil from his decrees, we can not but trust that he has been training, not only souls for heaven, but a nation to serve him in the land which he has given to them.

Another topic, to which we are bound to allude, however unwillingly, in treating of the adverse or discouraging circumstances in connection with Hawaiian Christianity, is that of divided religious interests. In the older portions of Christendom, the phenomenon of rival sects is understood, and their common appeal to the same plenary and divine authority casts the weight of their combined testimony and influence on the side of faith. But those recently converted from heathenism, accustomed to uniformity of belief and worship in their previous estate, and knowing little of the history of the Christian church, are perplexed and often thrown into scepticism by the antagonisms of mutually exclusive sects. They can not comprehend the identity of religion where there is no community of religious interest and feeling. In their view the denial of the doctrines and the contempt of the ritual in which they have been trained are tantamount to the rejection and contempt of Christianity. Even in the age of the apostles, and under the ministry of those who had received their doctrine from the lips or by the revelation of the Lord, it was feared lest different modes of teaching and discipline on the same soil might be fraught with mischief. St. Paul expresses his determination not to enter on other men's labors, and laments and deprecates the consequences of the intrusion on his own ground of teachers not authorized or approved by himself. In the world-wide field open to the philanthropy of the church, modern Protestant missionaries have in general recognized this principle, and have been unwilling to present before heathendom the spectacle of a distracted church and a divided Gospel. When they could not labor side by side without collision or wide dissiliency of aim or action, they have, like Abraham and Lot, fed their flocks apart.

This Christian comity has been violated by the Mission of the English church, or, as it styles itself, the " Reformed Catholic Mission." The subject is one which we would gladly omit; but we should do injustice equally to the work under review and to the mission cause, were we to pass it over in silence.

The late king having become interested in the services of the English church, and there being at Honolulu many English residents who had been educated in its worship, application was made by Rev. Dr. Armstrong, once a missionary of the American Board, and then filling the office of President of the Board of Public Instruction, and Mr. Wyllie, an Englishman, Minister of Foreign Affairs, to Rev. William Ellis of London, pledging a moderate salary to some suitable English clergyman, who might consent to assume the pastorate of a church at the capital. The request was made for "a man with evangelical sentiment, of respectable talents, and most exemplary Christian life. A high churchman," added Dr. Armstrong, " or one of loose Christian habits, would not succeed. He would not have the sympathy and support of the other evangelical ministers at all, but rather opposition." This application was in entire accordance with the wishes of the missionaries and their friends, Indeed Dr. Anderson had previously urged a bishop of the American Episcopal church to sent out a presbyter of his diocese with reference to such a charge. Mr. Wyllie, who seems to have been playing a double game, had previously entered into correspondence with Mr. Hopkins, the Hawaiian consul in London, and a plan was matured through his agency for sending to the Islands a bishop and three presbyters, under the [high church] auspices of the Society for Propagating the Gospel. When this project became known, the American Board instituted a correspondence with the Archbishop of Canterbury and the Bishop of London, both of whom are understood to have sympathized with the views of the Board, and to have been opposed to intrusion on the field which they had made their own. But the counsels of the high church party prevailed. Bishop Staley was consecrated in 1861, and arrived at Honolulu, accompanied by two of his presbyters, and shortly followed by a third, in October, 1862.

These men of lofty apostolic pretensions have taken precisely the course which might have been anticipated, and will undoubtedly succeed in creating schism and animosity among the native Christians. They ignore the ministerial character and office of the American missionaries. They avail themselves of every opportunity of baptising children, without reference to the ecclesiastical relations of the parents. They have established the most showy and Romeward tending modes of worship, "with surplice and stole, with alb, and cope, and crosier; with rochet, and mitre, and pastoral staff; with Episcopal ring and banner; with pictures, altar-candles, robings, intonations, processions and attitudes." Meanwhile Bishop Staley has been preaching the most extreme and offensive doctrines of his party in the church, doctrines diametrically opposed to those taught by the missionaries, patristical tradition, baptismal regeneration, the gift of the Holy Spirit in confirmation, confession to the priest, and priestly absolution. At the same time he has stultified himself, while he has no doubt mystified his serious hearers, and encouraged the undevout in the desecration of holy time, by declaring that Sunday is "most-falsely and mischievously called the Sabbath," and intimating that the daily service of the church and the observance of its solemn festivals fitly supersede the special reverence with which the people had been taught by the missionaries and required by the law of the land to regard the one day in seven. He has stultified himself, we say; for, unless the high church "has changed all this," the precept, "Remember that thou keep holy the Sabbath day," is read constantly in the ante-communion service, with the response, "Lord, have mercy upon us, and incline our hearts to keep this law." If Sunday is "most falsely and mischievously called the Sabbath," to what observance does this portion of the English liturgy have reference? Or does Bishop Staley require his adherents, in the most sacred service of the altar, to perform an act of solemn mockery, to offer a prayer which is arrant blasphemy, to beg of the divine mercy that they may be inclined to practice "falsehood and mischief"? Candles at noonday are a harmless folly; this is gross impiety.

The success of this mission has as yet been very limited. Its congregations are small. The modes of worship repel the simple tastes of such as have been sincerely attached to the ministrations of their earlier teachers; and those who want to be addressed through the senses, and gravitate toward the old idolatry, can find more that is congenial among the Roman Catholics than among their imitators. Yet under the patronage of the court and of some of the more influential foreign residents this superstition must needs grow. It can hardly fail to create a diversion from the interests of a simple faith and worship, which is especially to be deprecated at the present crisis, when the autonomy of the native church is just beginning, and needs the combined zeal, effort and liberality of all who love the cause of Christ and seek the prosperity of Zion.

We have spoken freely and warmly of this intrusion; but we believe that we have said no more than candid Episcopalians would readily admit and endorse. For the English church and its American sister we cherish all due reverence, gratitude and affection; and because we feel this, we can not think or write with easy tolerance of the stilted and popinjay caricatures of its solemn order and majestic ritual.

There is also on the Islands a Roman Catholic Mission, numbering as proselytes, (including all baptized persons,) more than twenty thousand souls. The Mormons have, too, a small settlement on the island of Lanai, and reckon, (including children,) not far from four thousand members. It does not appear that either of these forms of belief is making rapid progress, or presents any active hostility to the success of Protestant Christianity.

While we should be gratified to see this new-born people united in faith and worship, we can conceive that this diversity of ministration, these forms of error, these tares growing with the wheat, may be made subservient to their better proficiency in divine things. Inquiry, comparison, mental activity on religious subjects will be aroused and guided; the native pastors will feel the more intense need of taking heed to themselves, their doctrine and their flocks, because they are in the midst of gainsayers; private Christians will have added inducements to be loyal to the Master who can receive no wounds so deep as in the house of his friends; and thus a more intelligent faith and a more fervent piety may spring from the present division, and may prepare the way for the ultimate triumph of the truth over all obstacles and hindrances.

We have foreborne making extracts from the work under review, because we are unwilling that any of our readers should become acquainted with it in scraps or fragments. We have not even given an analysis of it, though our materials have been chiefly derived from it. Besides, there are no *especially* interesting extracts. The whole, from the Preface to the Appendix, is full of intense interest for all who love their Saviour and their race. The narrative flags not for one moment on the eager attention of the reader, nor can it fail to lift the devout heart as with a continuous anthem of praise to Him who has "given such power unto men," as is shown forth in this regenerated people.

One thought suggests itself in conclusion. Much of the science of our day busies itself, with a depraved ingenuity, in detaching man's hold on the ancestral tree by which he traces his descent from God, and of which, among the progeny of the second Adam, he may become a living branch. The true answer to these speculations is not to be found in ethnology or in physiology. No race can make out an unbroken pedigree; nor yet can we deny that there are strong analogies between the higher orders of quadrupeds and the lower members of the human family, not only in physical structure, but in mental capacity. Fifty years ago, the half-reasoning elephant or the tractable and troth-keeping dog might have seemed the peer, or more, of the unreasoning and conscienceless Hawaiian. From that very race, from that very generation, with which the nobler brutes might have scorned to claim kindred, have been developed the peers of saints and angels. Does not the susceptibility of regeneration, the capacity for all that is tender, beautiful and glorious in the humanity of the Lord from heaven — inherent in the lowest types of our race — of itself constitute an impassable line of demarcation between the brute and man? Has physical science a right to leave "the new man in Christ Jesus," which the most squalid savage may become, out of the question in its theories of natural selection or spontaneous development? When the modern Lucretianism can account for the phenomena of Christian salvation, without the intervention of miracle, revelation, or Redeemer, and not till then, can it demand our respect as a tenable theory of the universe.

# BARTIMEUS, THE BLIND PREACHER OF MAUI.*

### AS A PAGAN.

KAPIOLANI† belonged to the ruling class, but Bartimeus, of whom some account is now to be given, was from the lowest order of Hawaiian society. Yet he became a scarcely less distinguished trophy of divine grace. He was born on East Maui, about the year 1785. Pagan mothers on those islands then frequently destroyed their infant children to avoid the trouble of bringing them up, and it is said that Pu-a-a-i-ki‡ (which was his heathen name) would have been buried alive, but for the intervention of a relative. His birth was only a few years after the death of Captain Cook, the discoverer of the islands, and about as long before the visit of Vancouver. Not a ray of gospel light had then reached that beautiful cluster of islands. The inhabitants were all idolaters, and their altars were often stained with the blood of human victims. The people were ignorant and degraded, and were wasting under the influence of the most abominable vices. Puaaiki was as vicious and degraded as the rest. He early acquired a love for the intoxicating *awa;* and it is supposed that his blindness may have resulted from this, in connection with his filthy habits, and the burning tropical sun beating upon his bare head and unsheltered eyes. Before losing his sight, he had learned the *lua*, or art of murdering and robbery; the *kake*, a secret dialect valued for amusement and intrigue; and the *hula*, a combination of rude, lascivious songs and dances.

When the American mission reached Kailua in 1820, he was there in the king's train, playing the buffoon for the amusement of the queen and chiefs, and thus he obtained the means of subsistence. It is not probable that he knew any thing of the missionaries at that time. The royal family removed to Honolulu early in 1821, and the blind dancer made part of their wild and noisy train. There he suffered from illness, destitution, and neglect, and in his distress was visited by John Honolii, one of the Christian islanders brought by the mission from America, who spoke to him of the Great Physician. This interested him, and as soon as he could walk, he went with Honolii to hear the preaching of the missionaries. The impression he made on them was that of extreme degradation and wretchedness. His diminutive frame bowed by sickness, his scanty covering of bark-cloth, only a narrow strip around his waist and a piece thrown over his shoulders, his meagre face, his ruined eyes, his long black beard, his feeble, swarthy limbs, and his dark

---

* Two Memoirs of Bartimeus have been published in this country; one by the Massachusetts Sabbath-School Society in 1843, 16mo, pp. 126, prepared by the Rev. Jonathan S. Green, of the Sandwich Islands Mission; the other by the American Tract Society, (New-York) prepared by the Rev. Hiram Bingham, one of the pioneer missionaries to those islands, pp. 58, but without date. The materials for this article are drawn chiefly from the more extended notices by those veteran missionaries.

† See the May No. of Hours at Home for an interesting sketch of Kapiolani, by Dr. Anderson.—EDITOR.

‡ Pronounced Poo-ah-ah-ee-kee.

soul—all made him a most pitiable object.

### HIS CONVERSION.

Yet he was a chosen vessel, and Jesus was such a Friend and Saviour as he needed. Led by a heathen lad, he came often to the place of Christian worship, gave up his intoxicating drinks and the *hula*, and sought to conform to the rules of the gospel as he understood them. His heart was gradually opened, and the Spirit took of the things of Christ and showed them unto him. When now the proud chiefs again called for him to *hula* for their amusement, his reply was, "*That* service of Satan is ended; I intend to serve Jehovah, the king of heaven." He was rising on the scale of being. Some derided him, but some of high rank, and among them his patron the queen, were so far under the influence of the gospel, that they respected him for the stand he had taken. He even exhorted the queen to seek earnestly the salvation of her soul, and his exhortations seem not to have been wholly in vain.

The progress of Puaaiki in divine knowledge can be accounted for only by the teaching of the Spirit. His blindness did indeed favor his giving undivided attention as a hearer, and also the exercise of his powers of reflection and memory. His habit was to treasure up what he could of every sermon, and afterward to rehearse it to his acquaintances. It was thus he grew in knowledge, and at length became himself a preacher. "In the fourth year of the mission," says Mr. Bingham, "among the twenty-four chiefs and five hundred others then under our instruction, though there were marked and happy cases of advancement, none seemed to have gone further in spiritual knowledge than Puaaiki."

In March, 1823, he accompanied the native governor of Maui and his wife to Lahaina, on his native island. His patron, the governor, died in the following November, but Messrs. Richards and Stewart, missionaries, who had arrived a few months previously, then became his religious guides. In the summer of 1824, an insurrection occurred on the island of Kauai, the most northern of the group, which was soon suppressed; but it was followed by a sort of insurrectionary effort on the part of a heathen party on Maui, to revive some of the old idolatrous rites. Puaaiki and his associates, then known as "the praying ones," earnestly opposed this; and being called together by the missionaries, and instructed and encouraged, the blind convert was requested to lead in prayer. Mr. Stewart gives the following account of his own emotions occasioned by that prayer: "His petitions were made with a pathos of feeling, a fervency of spirit, a fluency and propriety of diction, and above all, a humility of soul, that plainly told he was no stranger there. His bending posture, his clasped hands, his elevated but sightless countenance, the peculiar emphasis with which he uttered the exclamation, 'O Jehovah,' his tenderness, his importunity, made us feel that he was praying to a God not afar off, but one that was nigh, even in the midst of us. His was a prayer not to be forgotten. It touched our very souls, and we believe would have touched the soul of any one not a stranger to the meltings of a pious heart."

### IS ADMITTED TO THE CHURCH.

It was not until the spring of 1825, that Puaaiki was received into the church. The missionaries seem to have erred on the side of caution, both in this case, and in that of Kapiolani. The darkness, pollution, and chaotic state of society, was the reason, though perhaps that should have been a motive for receiving those little ones earlier into the fold. But Puaaiki's expression of desire to be united with the people of God in the spring of 1825, could not be any longer resisted, and he was carefully examined by Mr. Richards, as to his Christian knowledge and belief, and the evidences of a work of grace in his heart. The following is a translation of a portion of his replies.

"Why do you ask to be admitted to the church?"

"Because I love Jesus Christ, and I love you the missionaries, and desire to dwell in the fold of Christ, and join with you in eating the holy bread, and drinking the holy wine."

" What is the holy bread ?"

" It is the body of Christ, which he gave to save sinners."

" Do we then eat the body of Christ ?"

" No ; we eat the bread which represents his body ; and as we eat bread that our bodies may not die, so our souls love Jesus Christ and receive him for their Saviour, that they may not die."

" What is the holy wine ?"

" It is the blood of Christ, which was poured out on Calvary, in the land of Judea, to save us sinners."

" Do we then drink the blood of Christ ?"

" No ; but the wine represents his blood, just as the holy bread represents his body, and all those who go to Christ and trust in him, will have their sins washed away in his blood, and their souls saved forever in heaven."

" Why do you think it more suitable for you to join the church than others ?"

" Perhaps it is not. If it is not proper, you must tell me ; but I do greatly desire to dwell in the fold of Christ."

" Who do you think are proper persons to be received into the church ?"

" Those who have repented of their sins, and have new hearts."

" What is a new heart ?"

" One that loves God, and loves the word of God, and does not love sin and sinful ways."

" Why do you hope you have a new heart ?"

" The heart I now have is not like the one I formerly had. The one I have now is very bad. It is unbelieving and inclined to evil. But it is not like the one I formerly had. Yes, I think I have a new heart."

These answers are given as a sample. Mr. Richards declares the questions to have been all new to him, and that he answered them from his own knowledge, and not from having committed any catechism.

On the tenth of July, 1825, Puaaiki was admitted into the church at Lahaina, and received the name of *Batimea Lalana.*

The name Lalana (London) was added at his own suggestion, in accordance with a Hawaiian custom of noting events. It was designed to commemorate the then recent visit of his former patrons, the king and queen, to London, and their deaths in that city. We shall use only the former of the two names, giving it the English form, *Bartimeus.*

It is needless to say, that this young convert had ceased from the use of all alcoholic drinks, and of *awa,* long before his admission to the Christian church. But when a translation of Paul's epistles came afterward into his hands, and he read, " Prove all things ; hold fast that which is good ; abstain from that which is of evil character,"[*] he thought it his duty to relinquish also the use of tobacco.

The Rev. Jonathan S. Green came to Lahaina three years after Bartimeus's public profession of his faith, and abode there a few months, and bore a most favorable testimony concerning him, as a " consistent Christian, adorning in all things the doctrine of God his Saviour."

### RESIDENCE AT HILO.

In 1829, Bartimeus was persuaded to remove, with his wife, to Hilo, on the island of Hawaii. Here his field was wider and more necessitous than it had been at Lahaina. Several natives of talent and influence had there been hopefully converted, some of them through his influence. Among them was David Malo, a most active and promising youth. Moreover, Lahaina had been longer favored with the means of grace. At Hilo —since so wonderfully blessed with outpourings of the Spirit—though desirous of returning to Lahaina, he was persuaded to make his home for several years. The resident missionary at first, was Mr. Goodrich, the same who met Kapiolani at the volcano. In the following year, Kaahumanu, the ex-queen and regent of the islands, visited Hilo, and this extraordinary woman seconded the efforts of Bartimeus by her influence as a ruler, and still more by her example as a Christ-

---

[*] 2 Thes. v. 21, 22, rendered back from the Hawaiian into English.

ian. The cool climate of that windward district, its green fields, its clouded skies and frequent rains, exerted such a beneficial effect upon his eyes, that he made a painful and partially successful effort to learn to read ; but the effort aggravated the evil, and he reluctantly gave up the design. "The light of the body," says Mr. Clark, who spent a season at Hilo, "did not increase in proportion to the light of the mind. Through the sense of hearing he was adding rapidly to his knowledge of the way of life. Every text and nearly every sermon which he heard, was indelibly fixed in his mind. The portions of Scripture, which were then being printed in his native language, were made fast in the same way. By hearing them read a few times, they were fixed, word for word, chapter and verse."

Mr. Green removed to Hilo in 1831, and remained there a year and a half. He saw Bartimeus daily, became intimately acquainted with him as a man and a Christian, and bears the most favorable testimony as to the faithful coöperation of his native brother and fellow-laborer. Bartimeus never remitted his activity, attending little neighborhoood meetings, accompanying the missionary, visiting alone or accompanied by his wife or some native Christian brother, and receiving the many who came to his own house, attracted by his social and affectionate disposition, and by his copious and spiritual conversation.

RESIDENCE AT WAILUKU.

Some time in 1834, Bartimeus removed to Wailuku, on the island of Maui, where, and in the vicinity, he continued to reside during the eight or nine years till his death. Here he was once more, and during a part of the time, associated with Mr. Green, whose love for him and confidence in him, and admiration for his character, appear to have increased to the last. In 1837, there were manifest indications of the great awakening, which so wonderfully pervaded the group of islands in the following year. The infant church at Wailuku was revived. The

members confessed their sins, and sought for pardon through the blood of atonement. No one seemed more deeply penitent than Bartimeus. No one was more importunate in seeking for pardon, on his own account, and for his brethren, and for the impenitent. "And when," adds Mr. Green, "during most of the year 1838, the Spirit of God moved upon the mass of the population ; and caused multitudes to bow to the sceptre of the Son of God, the heart of the good old man seemed to overflow with joy, and he poured out the emotions of his soul in language not easily described. None but those who saw him during some of those interesting scenes can conceive the appearance of Bartimeus. No painter could do justice to the heaven-illuminated countenance of our friend. And yet no one that saw that glow, that index of unearthly joy, can cease to retain an affecting impression of it."

As a consequence of this outpouring of the Spirit, people resorted from all quarters to Wailuku, coming often a distance of fifteen or twenty miles, for instruction. But this could not long be ; the aged, the infirm, and the young could not come so far at all. The people, therefore, erected houses of worship in all the large districts of Maui, and it became a difficult question how to supply them with preachers. Messrs. Green and Armstrong did the best that seemed to them possible in the circumstances : they selected a class of their most devoted and talented church-members, and instructed them in the Scriptures, in the elements of moral science, and in church history. Bartimeus was a prominent member of this class. From our present point of view, it seems as if he ought, long before this time, to have been formally licensed to preach, if not ordained as an evangelist, or even as the pastor of a church. But the ideas of our missionary brethren at that early period developed slowly, in this direction. Bartimeus was now set apart formally to the office of deacon, or elder. This appears to have been early in 1839. It was not until three years after this, that he received a formal license as a preacher of the gospel. And it was not until February, 1843, the beginning of his last year on earth, that he was ordained as an evangelist—his services being then statedly required by the people of Honuaula, twenty miles from Wailuku.

"Thus," says his most intimate associate and biographer, Mr. Green, "was this good man sent forth by the church at Wailuku to labor in the destitute field of Honuaula and Kahikinui. Judging from his labors at Hilo, at Wailuku, and indeed at every place where he had spent any considerable time, there was much reason to hope that he would prove a rich blessing to the inhabitants of those districts. He entered upon his work with his accustomed ardor. He proclaimed the glad tidings of a Saviour's mercy in the house of God, by the wayside, and from house to house; and he sought by every method to win souls to Christ. On the arrival of Mr. Clark as pastor of the church at Wailuku, he went over to welcome him to his new sphere of labor, and spent a week or two. He also came through Kula, 'preaching as he went,' to Makawao, aided me in the labor preparatory to the administration of the Lord's Supper, and spent the Sabbath. He then resumed his labors at Honuaula. There, while toiling with cheerfulness and hope for Christ and his brethren according to the flesh, and while we were rejoicing in the belief that many would be savingly benefited by his instrumentality, he was arrested by sickness. The attack being severe, he returned to Wailuku, that he might procure medical aid, and also be near his brethren with whom he had spent many years of delightful Christian intercourse. He seemed to have a presentiment from the commencement of his sickness, that he should not recover. But the thought of death gave him no alarm. Why should it? He knew whom he had believed. On the Lord Jesus Christ he had, long before, cast himself for time and eternity. This surrender had been suc-

ceeded by a sweet peace. He had the hope of the Christian. True, he did not escape the buffetings of Satan. The Lord suffered him for a little season to be tried, that the sincerity of his profession, the genuineness of his hope, and the intensity of his love might be more apparent. Hence, probably, the reply which he made to his pastor, when asked how he felt in view of another world— 'I fear I am not prepared; my sins are very great.' When he turned away, so to speak, from the cross of Christ, to look at his own sinful heart, he seemed well nigh desponding; but a view, by faith, of his gracious Lord, bleeding, dying a propitiatory sacrifice for sinners, now, exalted at the right hand of the Majesty on high, ever living to intercede for His people, this, this dispelled his fears. This made the prospect of going to dwell with him, and to be forever like him, exceedingly desirable. Bartimeus did not say as much that might be called a dying testimony as many others have done. There was less need that he should do so. His daily conversation, his holy example, and his unremitted labors in the cause of his blessed Master, had borne ample testimony; and by these, he, being dead, yet speaketh. For a day or two before his decease, he sank under the force of disease, so that he was unable to converse much. He slept in death on Sabbath evening, September seventeenth, 1843, and entered, as there is the most cheering reason to believe, into the rest which remaineth for the people of God."

"On the nineteenth," writes Mr. Clark, "his funeral was attended by a large congregation of sincere mourners. The voice, which had so·often been heard among us in devout supplication, and in earnest entreaty, calling the sinner to repentance, was silent in death. His purified spirit, raised from the darkest heathenism, by the blessing of God on missionary labor, was at peace with the Saviour, and all that was mortal was about to be committed to the dust to await the last trumpet. A sermon was preached from 2 Cor. v. 1 : "For we know that if our earthly house of this tabernacle were dissolved, we have a building of God, a house not made with hands, eternal in the heavens."

### HIS PROMINENT CHARACTERISTICS.

The character of Bartimeus shines out so clearly in the foregoing narrative, that little more need be said. His calling to be a preacher was evidently of God. He had original endowments for that service. There has been already some reference to the strength of his memory, and to his eloquence. An illustration of both is given by Mr. Clark, writing from Wailuku soon after his decease.

"In January last, I met him at a protracted meeting in this place, and was then more than ever impressed with the extent and accuracy of his knowledge of the Scriptures. He was called upon to preach at an evening meeting. His heart was glowing with love for souls. The overwhelming destruction of the impenitent seemed to be pressing with great weight upon his mind; and this he took for the subject of his discourse at the evening meeting. He chose for the foundation of his remarks, Jer. iv. 13. "Behold he shall come up as clouds, and his chariots shall be as a whirlwind." The anger of the Lord against the wicked, and the terrible overthrow of all his enemies, were portrayed in vivid colors. He seized upon the terrific image of a whirlwind or tornado as an emblem of the ruin which God would bring upon his enemies. This image he presented in all its majestic and awful aspects, enforcing his remarks with such passages as Ps. lviii. 9: "He shall take them away as with a whirlwind, both living, and in his wrath;" Prov. i. 27: "And your destruction cometh as a whirlwind;" Isa. xl. 24: "And the whirlwind shall take them away as stubble;" Jer. xxx. 23: "Behold the whirlwind of the Lord goeth forth with fury, a continuing whirlwind; it shall fall with pain upon the head of the wicked;" Hosea viii. 7: "For they have sown the wind, and they shall reap the whirlwind;" Nahum i. 3, Zech. vii. 14. and other passages in which the

same image is presented—always quoting chapter and verse. I was surprised to find that this image is so often used by the sacred writers. And how this blind man, never having used a Concordance or a Reference Bible in his life, could, on the spur of the moment, refer to all these texts, was quite a mystery. But his mind was stored with the precious treasure, and in such order that he always had it at command. Never have I been so forcibly impressed, as while listening to this address, with the remark of the Apostle, 'Knowing, therefore, the terror of the Lord, we persuade men;' and seldom have I witnessed a specimen of more genuine eloquence. Near the close he said, 'Who can withstand the fury of the Lord, when he comes in his chariots of whirlwind? You have heard of the cars in America, propelled by fire and steam, with what mighty speed they go, and how they crush all in their way; so will the swift chariots of Jehovah overwhelm all his enemies. Flee then to the ark of safety.'"

Mr. Armstrong who was with him five years, bears this remarkable testimony to his eloquence: "Often while listening with exquisite delight to his eloquent strains, have I thought of Wirt's description of the celebrated blind preacher of Virginia." "He is a short man and rather corpulent, very inferior in appearance when sitting, but when he rises to speak, he looks well, stands erect, gesticulates with freedom, and pours forth, as he becomes animated, words in torrents. He is perfectly familiar with the former, as well as the present, religion, customs, modes of thinking, and in fact the whole history of the islanders, which enables him often to draw comparisons, make allusions, and direct appeals, with a power which no foreigner will ever possess."

Mr. Clark thinks him more distinguished for his humility even, than for his eloquence. "Among all the graces which shone in him in such beautiful proportion, humility was the most conspicuous. Although much noticed by chiefs and missionaries, as well as those of his own rank, and occasionally receiving tokens of respect even from a far distant land, he was always the same. He sought the lowest place, and always exhibited the same modest demeanor, and appeared in the same humble garb. His prayer was, 'Lord be merciful to me a sinner.' This was the more remarkable, as it was in strong contrast to the natural character of Hawaiians. Although he labored for some time as a licensed preacher of the gospel, he probably never took his station in the pulpit while addressing an audience. He preferred a more humble position."

What shall we think of the capabilities of a race which produces such a man, and of the power of the gospel, when we trace the history of this Blind Preacher? And what value shall we place upon the results of the gospel on those islands, and upon the mission which justly reckons such results as among the fruits of its labors?